Summer Recipes

Healthy Recipes for Healthy Living

Doris C. Moore

# CAKES

The fact that soda and cream of tartar are the ingredients of the best baking powders is well understood.

Dr. Lillis Wood Starr says: "Cream of tartar belongs to the same class with soda. Soda is bi-carbonate of sodium; cream of tartar is bi-tartrate of potassium. Sodium, potassium and calcium (lime) all belong to the same group of metals and are injurious to the tissues of our bodies."

Dr. Lauretta Kress—"Cream of tartar or Potassium Bi-tartrate is a gastro-intestinal irritant like soda. By combining cream of tartar and soda, we have Rochelle salts. If needed as a cathartic, they are better given as such on an empty stomach; then the system quickly gets rid of them. If taken in food they are retained longer and become more irritating."

"Sugar when largely used is more injurious than meat."

Cake at its best is not to be recommended, but for those who have not yet discarded it, we give a variety of recipes for cakes without baking powder or soda: there are some, also, without eggs.

When a few more eggs are used in a cake than would be required with chemicals, remember that less of the nitrogenous is necessary in other dishes: also, that the health of your family is of the first importance and it would be better not to give them any cake at all than that which will poison their systems.

## Suggestions

Use pastry flour for all cakes; and since different brands even of pastry flour differ, it is best to use the same brand when you find a good one and become accustomed to it.

Sift flour once before measuring; and from 3–5 times for angel and other sponge cakes after measuring. The best way to sift flour several times is to lay down two pieces of large letter or Manila paper and to sift the flour first on to one and then on to the other.

All measurements have the sifted flour laid lightly into the cup with a spoon. If the cup is shaken or knocked on the side with the spoon there will be too much flour.

Skimmed milk and oil may be used in cakes and the cream saved for other purposes.

At great altitude, more flour and less shortening and sugar will be required in cakes.

In recipes calling for cream of tarter, use lemon juice in the proportion of 1 tablespn. or more to each teaspoon of cream of tartar. A larger quantity of lemon juice makes the cake more tender.

2 whites of eggs are said to equal 1 rounded teaspn. of baking powder, for lightness.

Boil molasses or syrup before using in cakes.

Half oil instead of all butter may be used in nearly all cakes, and in some cases, all oil is better. Use salt with oil.

It is usually thought important to cream butter and sugar well together, but one professional cake-maker told me that cakes were lighter when the butter and sugar were just mixed.

Always add a little of the flour for cakes to the creamed butter or sugar and butter, before adding eggs, milk or other liquids.

Saffron is used for both color and flavor: a very small quantity only, is required of the imported for a deep color.

For variety, thin slices of sweet prunes or dates are nice in place of other fruits in cakes.

Round tube pans bake cake the most evenly, Turk's head molds being the best of all.

Do not oil the tins, for cakes without shortening.

For cakes with shortening, oil the tins and sprinkle flour over, shaking off all flour that is loose; or, line tins with well oiled paper.

Some recommend dipping angel cake pans into cold water and filling while wet; then the cake falls out white when cold, leaving the crust sticking to the mold.

Always beat whites of eggs on a platter or in a large cake bowl or "bombe" with a whip, not with a revolving beater.

Chop and fold, never stir, the whites into cake, the flour also.

Have all ingredients and utensils for sponge cake cold, and if possible, put it together in a cold room.

For sponge cakes, follow directions for putting nut and citron cake together, or the hot water way following sponge layer cake.

Bake sponge cakes very slowly and evenly in an oven that bakes well from the bottom. They will retain their lightness better if carefully inverted in the tin after baking and left in that position until cool.

Bake cakes with shortening in a moderate oven.

Cool all cakes slowly. One colored cook told me that she always set her cakes on the stove hearth for a little while after taking them out of the oven. Of course they should be handled carefully.

Set warm layer and other cakes on a cloth wrung out of cold water and they will quickly loosen from the pan.

Loaf or layer cakes may be set in ice box in tins for 2 hrs. before baking.

3 or 4 rose geranium leaves laid in the bottom of the tin before the batter is poured in will flavor cake with rose, or the leaves may be laid between layers after baking, while cooling. If the loaf is one that will bear removing from the tin while warm, lay it on some of the leaves.

Cakes may be steamed instead of baked—sponge cakes 1 hour, fruit cakes longer. One recipe for fruit cake says, steam 4 hours and bake 1 hour. Use your judgment.

Sponge cakes—angel and others, are supposed to be broken apart with 2 forks, not cut.

If loaves of cake that are to be covered with whipped cream are cut before the cream is put on, the cake will look smooth and nice and the pieces will come out more neatly.

Cakes made with yeast require to be kept a little warmer than bread (unless you keep bread too warm), and flour, fruit and all ingredients should be warm when added.

## ★Nut and Citron Cake

3 large or 4 small eggs

1 scant cup granulated sugar

1 tablespn. lemon juice

1 tablespn. ice water

⅔–¾ cup Brazil nut, almond, pecan or shell-bark meal

½ cup (¼ lb.) fine chopped or ground citron

1 cup pastry flour

salt

Have all the ingredients as nearly ice cold as possible; sift the sugar, sift the flour twice and leave it in the sifter; beat the yolks of the eggs in a cake bowl with a revolving egg-beater (a large one if you have it), adding sugar gradually. When stiff, add part of the water and more sugar; beat, add more water, sugar and half the lemon juice, beating, until all the sugar is in.

Stir into this mixture half the nut meal, a pinch of salt and the citron. Rest the egg beater on a quart measure (or some dish of the required height) by the side of the bowl, and let it drain into the bowl while beating the whites of the eggs. It will drain much cleaner than it could be scraped, besides saving the time. Beat the whites of the eggs to a moderately stiff froth, add the remaining half tablespn. of lemon juice and whip till dry and feathery; let them stand a moment, then slide onto the yolk mixture; sprinkle part of the nut meal over them and sift on a little flour; chop in lightly, dipping from the bottom with a large thin spoon three times; add more meal and flour; chop; continue this until the flour is all in. Take care not to mix too much; the mixture must not get soft. Put into pan at once and bake slowly until the cake stops singing, or does not stick to a broom splint. Bake 1½ hours, according to the heat of the oven. The fine particles of citron give an unusually delightful flavor to the cake. Preserved orange peel, ground, may be used sometimes; or fine cut raisins or dried blueberries.

## ★Julia' sBirthdayCake

2 cups sugar
½–1 cup butter
8 eggs
2 cups flour
flavoring

Cream butter and sugar; add flavoring and a little of the flour, then the beaten yolks; beat well. Slide the stiffly-beaten whites on to this mixture, sift flour over gradually and chop together as for nut and citron cake; bake in moderate oven in 3 medium sized layers; sift a little sugar over one layer before baking, sometimes, to make a crust for the top. If possible, set in ice box for an hour before baking.

### PattyCakes

Use ⅓–½ cup of milk and 2½–2¾ cups of flour in preceding recipe, and bake in patty pans.

### CocoanutLoaforLayerCake

2 cups sugar

4 level tablespns. butter

8 eggs

2 cups fine grated or ground cocoanut

2 teaspns. lemon juice

1–2 teaspns. vanilla if desired

2 cups flour

Put together the same as "Julia's Birthday Cake," let stand on ice for 2 hours, or bake at once in loaf or layers.

If baked in layers, use Washington pie filling with it.

### RichLoafCake

1 cup butter

1⅔ cup granulated sugar

5 eggs

2–2¼ cups flour

Cream butter, add sugar and work very light; add 1 egg at a time and stir only until no yolk can be seen; mix in flour, turn into paper-lined pan and set in ice box for 2 hours. Bake in slow oven about an hour, or until the cake stops singing.

### RiceFlourCake

¾ cup butter

2 scant cups sugar

2¼ cups rice flour

6 eggs

2–3 tablespns. lemon juice with grated rind

Cream butter, add sugar, a little of the flour and beaten yolks with half the juice and all the rind of lemon.

Beat whites of eggs with a little salt, adding the remainder of the lemon juice when half beaten; slip on to cake batter, sift flour over gradually, and fold all lightly together. Put into pan to depth of not over 2 in. Bake in moderate oven.

### FruitandNutCake.Unsurpassed

1⅓ cup sugar

⅔ cup butter

1⅓ cup flour

6 eggs

4 cups (1⅓ lb.) seeded raisins

3 cups (1 lb.) currants

1½ cup (½ lb.) ground citron

large ¾ cup blanched almonds, ground

¼–½ teaspn. extract rose, according to strength

(rose leaves in their season)

Mix fruit with part of the flour, add nuts; cream butter with a little of the flour; beat together the sugar and yolks of eggs until very light and add with extract to creamed butter; beat well; whip whites of eggs with pinch of salt to stiff froth, add fruit and nuts to yolk mixture, chop in beaten whites and remainder of flour; bake in well oiled tin 1½–2½ hrs. in moderate and slow oven; cover when necessary.

The cake may be steamed 3–4 hrs. and baked ½–1 hr.

This cake will keep a long time with care and is unusually desirable. 3 times the quantity given will make 4 medium sized loaves.

## CornStar chCake

6 eggs

½ cup butter (part oil)

1⅓ cup sugar

1½ cup flour

3 tablespns. corn starch

flavoring

Beat yolks with half the sugar and cream butter with the other half; mix, beat. (Part of the flour and corn starch may be added to the butter and sugar.) Beat whites of eggs stiff, slide on to the mixture, add flour and corn starch (which have been sifted together) gradually, chopping and folding in with the whites; bake in moderate oven. Two thick round layers.

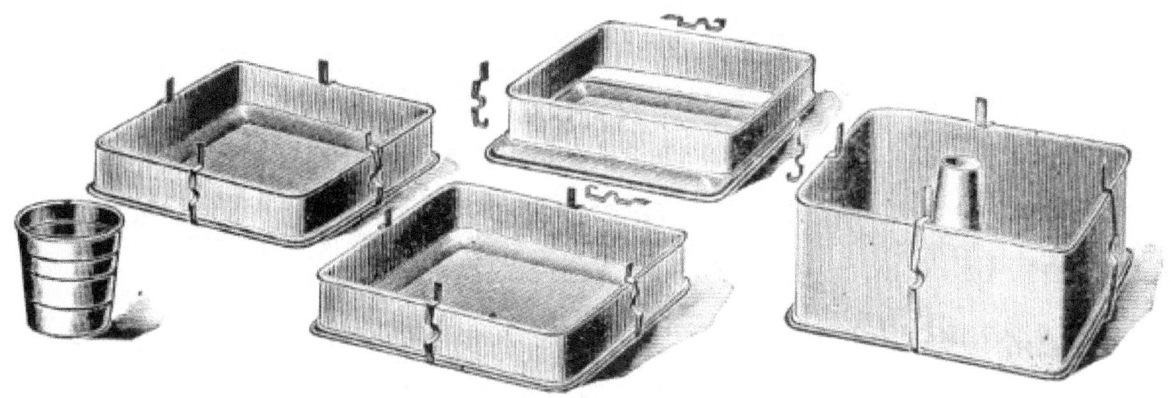

THE MISSES LISK CAKE TINS

### ★SilverCake

1 lb. (2 cups and 3 tablespns.) sugar

¾ lb. (3⅛–3½ cups) flour

6 oz. (¾ cup soft) butter

rose flavor

1½ cup citron or prunes in slices

whites of 14 eggs

Cream butter and sugar, add flavoring, beaten whites and flour, lay slices of fruit in and on top of cake. One very large square, or two rather small round loaves.

### ★ScotchShortBr ead—noeggs

½ cup butter

½ cup granulated or brown, or slightly rounded ½ cup powdered sugar

1 teaspn. caraway seed or not

2 cups flour

Cream butter, add sugar and flour mixed, seeds also if used. A little of the flour may be saved for rolling.

Roll to about 1 in. thick, of the shape to fit your tin; crinkle the edges, press them with a fork or cut with pastry jagger, slide on to tin, prick lightly with fork and bake in a slow oven for 1 hour; or, roll ½ in. thick and bake ½ hour only. The cake is sometimes creased in squares before baking, or the dough may be cut in round cakes and the edges crinkled.

The cake is better with oil and ¼ teaspn. of salt in place of butter. One cup of sugar is sometimes used with ½ cup of butter or oil, and again, 1 cup of butter or oil with ½ cup of sugar, but the cake is very nice with the proportions given. By some, brown sugar is considered most suitable.

### GermanLightCake

1⅛ cup butter or 1¼ cup oil
1¼ cup granulated sugar
2½–2¾ cups flour
⅞ cup almonds, blanched and chopped
4 eggs
grated orange rind
ground coriander seed

Cream butter with a little flour, add eggs, one at a time, beating, add sugar (except a little for the top), rind and flour; spread thin in oiled pans, sprinkle with almonds, coriander and sugar, bake in moderate oven, cut in squares while hot, leave in pan to cool.

### ★SisterElliott'sPlainLoafCakeandCookies

½ cup oil
1½ cup sugar
yolks 2 eggs

4½ cups flour
1 cup milk
salt, flavoring
whites 3 eggs

Cream oil and sugar, add a little flour, yolks of eggs, salt and flavoring, then milk and flour alternately; beat well and fold in the stiff whites of eggs. Chill, or bake at once thoroughly, in 1 large or 2 small loaves in moderate oven that bakes well from the bottom.

For cookies, use 2 whites of eggs only and make dough stiff enough to roll.

### MolassesCake

4 large eggs
3 level tablespns. butter
½ cup molasses
½ cup sugar, brown or white
1 teaspn. lemon juice
1½ teaspn. grated orange peel
1½ tablespn. browned flour
1 cup pastry flour

Beat eggs and lemon juice in bowl set in boiling water, add sugar, then boiling molasses, with butter and orange peel, and lastly the flour.

### MolassesSugarCakes

4 eggs
⅓ cup (4½ level tablespns.) butter

⅞ cup molasses sugar

⅓ teaspn. lemon extract

1 cup pastry flour

1½ tablespn. browned flour

1 teaspn. lemon juice

Mix butter and sugar and add to beaten yolks, beating well; slide on to this the whites beaten with salt and lemon juice, then sift over gradually the two flours mixed, chopping and folding them in with the whites. Bake in small cakes in moderate oven 15–20 m. Use grated maple sugar for maple cakes.

### ★Molasses Bread or Hard Molasses Cake—no eggs

1¾ qt. (7 cups) flour

1 cup butter (part oil)

1¼ cup pressed down, medium brown sugar

1 cup molasses

1 teaspn. ground anise seed

salt

Cream butter and sugar, add anise and molasses, beat well and add flour; turn mixture out on floured board, mold up and put into flat tins about 1 in. deep, wash over with milk and bake in a very slow oven.

When done, wrap or cover with damp cloths and keep at least 4 days before using. If necessary, moisten the cloths again, and perhaps again. The cakes will be hard and dry when taken from the oven, but keeping them for a few days in damp (not wet) cloths makes them nice and tender. Grated orange peel and vanilla, together or separate, may be used for flavoring; but the delicate flavor of anise is especially agreeable.

By weight, the ingredients are 1½ lb. pastry flour, ½ lb. butter, ½ lb. brown sugar, ⅞ lb. molasses.

## YEASTCAKES

It is especially important to use pastry flour in cakes made with yeast.

A good liquid yeast gives better results in cake, but compressed yeast may be used.

### ★Saffr onCake—noeggs

2 cups milk

4 tablespns. yeast

8½ cups flour

2 cups (1 lb.) butter

2½ cups sugar

¼ cup domestic saffron, not more than 1 teaspn. of imported

1 cup water in which saffron has been steeped ½ hr.

3 cups currants

2 cups fine cut or ground citron

1 teaspn. lemon extract

⅔–1 cake compressed yeast dissolved in a very little water, with sugar, may be used instead of soft yeast, and 1 extra tablespn. of water added to the sponge.

Make a sponge at night of the milk (just warm), yeast and 4½ cups of flour, and in the morning add the cup of warm saffron water. Cream the butter and sugar with a little flour, add the sponge gradually, mixing and beating, then the remainder of the flour warm (except a little which has been used to dust the fruit), beat well, add the extract and warmed, floured fruit, mix and pour into 3 good sized paper lined cake pans. Let stand until bubbles appear in the batter, usually 2–3 hrs. with soft yeast; not so long, perhaps, with compressed; when light, put into a slow oven; let cakes come up slowly and bake very moderately until they stop singing, 1½–2 hrs., depending upon the heat of the oven, but they must bake slowly.

When cake is started in the morning, 6 tablespns. of soft, or a whole cake of compressed yeast may be used. The quantity of flour may need to be varied a little according to the brand.

### Citron and Cocoanut Cakes—no eggs

1 cup milk

2 tablespns. yeast, (or ⅓–½ cake compressed yeast with extra ½ tablespn. of water in sponge)

4¼ cups flour

1 cup butter

1¼ cup sugar

½ cup water

¾–1 cup ground citron

¼ teaspn. weak extract rose

1 cup shredded cocoanut

1 teaspn. vanilla

Prepare as in preceding recipe (of which it is just half) and at the last divide into 2 parts, add the citron and rose to one, and the cocoanut and vanilla to the other. The loaves will not be very large.

### White Fruit Cake—no eggs

The whole of the above recipe, using only ¾ cup of butter, with ¾–1 cup of citron, 1 cup of cocoanut and ⅔ cup of almonds, all ground.

## ★DriedAppleCake—yeast

Cut 2 cups dried apples into small pieces with shears, soak over night in 1½ cup water, then cook in ¾ cup molasses until transparent.

*Sponge*—1 cup water, 1 cake compressed yeast, 2½ cups flour.

*When light,* add ⅔ cup butter (or half oil) and ½ cup sugar creamed together, the dried apples, grated rind of orange or lemon, 2 beaten eggs and 2 cups flour.

One egg only may be used; the cake is excellent with no eggs.

## ★WashingtonCake—noeggs

Remember to lay flour lightly into cup.

*Sponge—*
- 1 pt. milk
- 1 cake yeast
- ½ cup sugar
- 1 qt. flour

*When light—*
- salt
- 1–1¼ cup sugar
- 1 cup water in which a little saffron has been steeped
- 1½ cup oil and butter, half of each
- ¾–1 teaspn. lemon extract

6½ cups flour

Prepare same as saffron cake and bake in not too thick loaves.

## WashingtonPie—noeggs

Bake Washington cake in rather thin, flat loaf, split and put the following cream between and around, or put cream over and around cake without splitting.

*Cream—*
- 1½ tablespn. cooking oil
- 2½–2¾ tablespns. flour
- 1 pt. milk
- salt
- large ½ cup sugar
- yellow color
- 1 teaspn. vanilla

Heat oil, add flour, then hot milk, salt and sugar, stirring smooth at different stages. Steep a trifle of saffron in the milk. Add vanilla when cold.

*Another Cream—*
- 1 tablespn. butter
- 2½ tablespns. flour
- 1 pt. boiling milk
- ⅓ cup sugar
- salt
- 1 egg
- flavoring

## Elizabeth's Raised Cake

*Sponge—*
- 5–5¼ cups flour
- ½ cup sugar
- 2 tablespns. yeast (or ½ cake compressed yeast)
- 1½ cup milk

*When light—*
- 1½ cup sugar
- 1 cup butter
- 2 eggs
- 1 cup raisins
- ⅓ cup citron

Make sponge at night with soft yeast or early in the morning with compressed.

When light, add the butter, well creamed with the sugar, and beaten eggs. Beat all very thoroughly and put into the tins. When partly risen, stick the fruit in all over the top; let rise about 1½ hr., or until bubbles may be seen; bake 1 hr. in moderate oven. The cake is excellent without fruit.

## German Almond Loaf

*Sponge—*
- ¾ cup milk
- 3 tablespns. liquid yeast or 1 cake compressed yeast
- 3 cups flour

*When light—*

    4 yolks of eggs

    1 cup sugar

    ¾ cup butter

    ¾ cup of warm milk

    3–4 cups flour

    halved blanched almonds or halves of pecans or walnuts

    grated rind of 1–1½ lemon

Beat yolks with sugar and add to butter which has been creamed with part of the flour; then add the flavoring, the sponge, the milk and the flour alternating, beating until the flour is all in. Butter tube mold or other pans thick with cold butter and stick almonds to sides in regular rows. Do not put any in the bottom. Half fill pan with batter and let rise until pan is nearly full; bake 1 hr., or until cake stops singing, in moderate and slow oven so as not to burn nuts.

## CakeW ithoutChemicals
(Mrs. W. W. Wheeler, Ambato, Ecuador.)

    1 large cup thin bread sponge

    3 eggs, save out 1 white or yolk

    1 cup sugar

    5 tablespns. oil

    ⅔ cup flour

Beat eggs and sugar, add oil, then the sponge, lastly fold in the flour; put into 3 layer cake pans and let stand for 2 or 3 hours in a not very warm place. Bake in moderate oven.

Filling—Beat the white of egg stiff, add 1 tablespn. sugar and 2 tablespns. thick cream, or, make a cream sauce of the yolk.

### MapleLoafCake

1 cup bread dough
½ cup butter
1 egg
1 cup maple sugar

Cream the butter, add the sugar and beaten egg and mix all thoroughly with the dough; add a little flour, turn into tin and let rise ½ hr. or longer before baking.

### RaisedMolassesCake—noeggsortwowhites

*Sponge*—2 cups skimmed milk, 4 tablespns. yeast, 4½ cups flour.
*When light*—2 cups (1 lb.) butter, 2 cups molasses which has been boiled and cooled to lukewarm, 3 cups (not too fine) nuts, raisins, citron or cocoanut or combinations of same, 4–4½ cups flour, part for fruit. The whites of 2 eggs may be used with the 4 cups of flour.
Attend to sponge and cake as soon as light. Steam or bake.

### GermanCoffeeCake—noeggs

1 pt. milk
1 tablespn. butter
2 tablespns. sugar
½–1 cake compressed yeast
salt

flour for soft dough

Let rise, knead, spread on flat tin with floured hand, ¾–1 in. thick, spread with butter, sprinkle with sugar and ground coriander seed; or, spread with an egg beaten with a teaspn. of sugar, sprinkle with sugar and chopped or split blanched almonds; let rise; bake in moderate oven.

Use universal crust dough if a more tender cake is desired.

## ★RoyalSpongeCake

3 eggs

⅔ cup sugar

1 tablespn. lemon juice

1 tablespn. ice water

⅔ cup pastry flour

3 drops extract rose

Put together and bake same as nut and citron cake except for the nut meal. This makes 1 loaf or 2 small layers. 3 times the quantity makes 2 large square loaves, or 4 large layers.

May use 1½ tablespn. of orange juice with yolks of eggs and ½ tablespn. lemon juice with whites in place of the water and lemon juice. Flavor sugar with oil of orange and add ½ teaspn. vanilla to the cake. Finished with royal filling and icing, this makes a cake suitable for a royal occasion.

## VariationsofRoyalSpongeCake

(1) Use 2 tablespns. of cream in cake instead of lemon juice and water, with or without 1 teaspn. of lemon juice in whites of eggs.

(2) Use ⅔ cup of molasses in place of the sugar, no water, 1 teaspn. only, of lemon juice in the whites of eggs, 1 cup of flour and 1–2 teaspns. ground coriander seed.

(3) Use brown sugar in place of white, and orange or vanilla flavoring.

### ★SpongeLayerCake

3 eggs
1 cup sugar
4 tablespns. water
1–1½ cup flour

Boil sugar and water till syrup will thread, pour hot syrup slowly over beaten yolks; beat until cool, chop in stiffly-beaten whites and flour; flavor if desired. 2 small layers.

The sponge layer cake and all sponge cakes containing the yolks of eggs may be put together as follows: Break the eggs into a cake bowl, set the bowl into a pan of boiling water on the table and beat until light; add hot water (if any) and the sugar (or the hot syrup) gradually, beating. When light, remove from water, add flavoring and fold in flour lightly.

### ★OldFriendSpongeCake

1½ cup granulated sugar flavored with oil of lemon
large ½ cup cold water
7 eggs
1–1½ tablespn. lemon juice
2½ cups flour, sifted 5 or 6 times after measuring

Pour cold water over sugar, heat and boil slowly until perfectly clear; cool, beat yolks of eggs, add syrup and half the lemon juice and beat very light; slide whites of eggs beaten to a stiff froth with the remainder of the lemon juice on to mixture, sift flour over, a little at a time, and chop in with whites until all the flour is in. Bake ¾–1 hr. in slow oven until just done, no longer. 1 large loaf in deep square tin.

### CocoanutSpongeCake.1846

6 eggs

1 cup sugar

1 cup flour

a trifle of salt

1½ cup grated fresh cocoanut

lemon or vanilla flavoring

Put together as nut and citron cake, or beat eggs in dish set in hot water, add sugar, cocoanut and flavoring, then flour. Put mixture 1½ in. deep in pans lined with buttered paper.

### RiceFlourSpongeCake.1846

6 eggs

½ cup sugar

flavoring

⅔ cup rice flour

scant ⅓ cup pastry flour

Beat eggs in dish set in hot water, add sugar, flavoring and rice and pastry flour mixed. Bake in moderate oven.

## AngelCake

1 cup of egg whites 8 large or 10 small eggs

1¼ cup granulated or 1½ cup powdered sugar

1 cup flour

1–2 tablespns. lemon juice

a pinch of salt

1 teaspn. vanilla

Sift 2 or 3 cups of sugar twice; measure out 1 cup; sift a sifter of flour 4 times; measure out 1 cup and mix it with the cup of sugar; put both in the sifter and sift once, return to the sifter and set in cold place; separate the eggs, putting the whites into the dish in which they are to be beaten and set them in a cold place for 15–20 m.; when cool, add the salt to the eggs and begin beating with a long slow stroke, gradually increasing the velocity until the eggs begin to stiffen, then pour the lemon juice over and beat more rapidly for a time; continue beating until whites are stiff and feathery, then add flavoring; sift flour and sugar mixture over gradually, chopping and folding it in carefully; when all is in, drop by spoonfuls evenly into the pan and bake in slow oven 35–50 m., testing with broom straw. When done, turn the pan upside down with the sides resting on two saucers (unless you have the pans with projections for that purpose), so that a current of air will pass under and over the cake.

## Tri-ColoredLayerCake

Angel cake—½ white flavored with vanilla; ½ pink flavored with rose, 3 or 4 large layers. Other layers, of sponge layer cake lemon flavored, or some nice light brown cake such as molasses sugar cake or sponge layer cake with part browned flour. Filling of raisin dressing.

## Miss Lubey's Cream Puffs. 1 doz.

1 large cup boiling water
½ cup butter or oil
1 cup pastry flour
3 eggs
salt

Add dry flour all at once to boiling water and butter; stir quickly over the fire until mixture forms a ball which leaves the pan; remove from fire and stir till partly cool; add beaten yolks of eggs, part at a time, beating well, then slightly beaten whites; beat; set in cold place, covered, for 1 hr. or more; drop by spoonfuls about 2 in. apart on oiled and floured tin, flatten with brush or fingers dipped in milk (may leave without shaping); have oven rather quick at first, then slower until there is no "singing". Puffs are light weight when done. They will keep for several days. Reheat before filling. To fill, cut open at the side with shears.

The butter and flour may be creamed together first, and the boiling water poured over, then the whole cooked as before.

*Cream—*
1 pt. milk
½ cup sugar
1 tablespn. flour
2 eggs
salt
1 teaspn. vanilla

Mix sugar and flour, pour boiling milk over, boil up well; pour over beaten eggs, return to fire until just creamy, not boiling, cool; add salt and flavoring.

If cream is preferred thicker, use ½ cup of flour and cook in double boiler 15 m. before adding the eggs.

Whipped cream may be used for the filling, but does not harmonize as well with the shells.

These shells are sometimes used for trumese and celery salad, or for creamed meat dishes.

Dainty little puffs filled with different creams may be used for garnishes for desserts, or piled on fancy plates for cakes.

## AdditionstoCookiesandSmallCakes

Caraway or anise seeds, ground coriander or anise seed; chopped shelled nuts; grated or shredded cocoanut; grated orange or lemon rind; English currants; fine cut or ground raisins, citron, figs and dates; sometimes a raisin or half a blanched almond or half of a pecan or hickory nut meat in the center of each.

## SuggestiveCombinations

Coriander, English currants and English walnuts; raisins in molasses cookies; almonds chopped without blanching, and raisins; almonds same, and caraway or ground coriander seed.

Graham flour cookies with English currants; 1 part raisins and ⅓ part each of nuts, cocoanut and citron, with or without vanilla or lemon.

All cooky dough should be set in a cold place for 2 hrs. or longer before rolling out. Roll out in cool room on well floured board. Cut the cakes all out, put on tins and set in cold place before beginning to bake them as the baking will require all one's attention.

Very thin dough may be cut oblong, round or in any desired shape and some of the following fillings placed between each two pieces before they are baked—

Ground or mashed dates or figs rolled thin and cut with the same cutter that the dough was cut with; raspberry or other fruit jams and jellies or orange marmalade, also some of the suitable cake fillings.

It may sometimes be more convenient to cut the dough into strips 4 in. wide, spread half the width with the fruit, fold the other half over, pinch down the edge and cut into 3 in. lengths.

Tops of cookies may sometimes be brushed with white of egg and water or with syrup of ½ cup each sugar and water boiled together; or, sprinkled with sugar, coriander, chopped nuts or suitable fruits.

Instead of sprinkling cookies with different materials, brush the tops with milk and turn them on to any preparation or mixture desired.

Grated and sifted maple sugar may be used in place of other sugar in cookies by using a somewhat smaller quantity.

Oil and flour pans for baking cookies.

It is a good plan to bake cookies on the bottom of inverted dripping pans. This prevents them from burning on the bottom and it is easier to remove them from the tins.

## ★RichSmallCakes—Cookies

*(From an old recipe book of my auntie's, published in 1846)*

1 cup butter
scant 1¼ cup sugar
2⅔–2⅞ cups pastry flour
2 eggs
vanilla, almond or any desired flavoring

*By weight—*
    ½ lb. butter,
    ½ lb. sugar,
    10 ozs. flour.

Cream butter, add sugar, beaten eggs, flavoring and flour; let stand in cold place until thoroughly cold; roll ⅜–½ in. thick. Bake in oven which is moderately hot at first, so cakes will not spread. Be careful not to burn.

A little more flour may be used if preferred, also half oil instead of all butter, and brown sugar instead of granulated.

For *Jumbles*, break off pieces of dough the size of a walnut and make into rings by rolling out rolls as large as the finger and joining the ends; or, cut in rings; dust with sugar.

## YolkJumbles

    ¼ cup butter
    ½ cup sugar
    lemon flavoring
    yolks 4 eggs
    scant pint of flour
    salt

Poach yolks of eggs dry and mealy; rub them smooth and add butter gradually, creaming; add sugar and flavoring, then flour, a little at a time; cool, roll thin, cut with doughnut cutter, dust with sugar, bake.

## ★Cr eamCookies

    1½ cup sugar

1 cup thin cream
1 teaspn. vanilla
yolks of 3 eggs
scant ¾ cup butter and oil half and half
about 4½ cups flour

Cream butter and sugar, stir in a little flour, add beaten yolks, beat well, then add the cream gradually with the flavoring, and lastly, all of the flour. Handle after mixing the same as rich small cakes. Fruits, nuts or seeds maybe added. These cookies will keep almost indefinitely.

### Lunch Cakes

Take ½ the sugar and a little more flour in rich small cakes, or cream cookies, and roll to ½ or 1 in. in thickness. Cut of the size to fit tins, crinkle edges or press with fork, crease in squares and bake in moderate oven. Caraway or other flavoring may be used. Chopped nuts, a little sugar and ground or shredded citron may be mixed on a board or flat pan and one side of the cakes pressed into the mixture before baking. Set in cold place before rolling out.

### Anise Wafers, or German Christmas Cakes

½ cup butter
1 cup sugar
3 eggs
¾ teaspn. ground anise seed or 1 teaspn. whole seed
flour for soft dough

Cream butter, add sugar and a little flour, with seeds, then the yolks of the eggs, one at a time, and the stiffly-beaten whites, with flour, folding together lightly; knead in flour for soft dough, cover and set in cold place; roll rather thin, cut cakes about the size of a half dollar.

### Sour Cream Cookies—no soda

1½ cup sugar

1 cup thick sour cream

yolks 3 eggs

scant ¾ cup oil or butter

any desired flavoring, fruits nuts or seeds

5–5½ cups pastry flour

Mix lightly, set in cold place, roll rather thin.

### Honey Wafers

1 cup honey boiled and cooled

⅔ cup butter

2 small eggs or 1 large one

pinch salt

5 cups flour

Cream butter with a little flour, add beaten egg and honey, then remainder of flour.

### Molasses Cookies

¾ cup molasses

2 eggs

1 cup butter

½ cup granulated sugar

½–¾ teaspn. lemon extract

2 tablespns. browned flour

about 3½ cups pastry flour

Heat molasses to boiling and pour slowly, stirring, over well beaten eggs; cool; cream butter and sugar, stir in browned flour mixed with a little of the white flour, add flavoring with eggs and molasses, then the remainder of the flour or enough to make a not too soft dough. Set in cold place and roll out the same as small cakes. Care must be taken in baking, as molasses burns easily.

Or, boil and cool molasses, cream butter and sugar, add beaten eggs, a little flour, then molasses gradually, beating well, and finally, the flour.

Browned flour may be omitted and a few drops of rose extract used in flavoring.

### ★MolassesCakes—noeggs

1¼ cup oil or butter

2 cups molasses

orange or lemon rind or

coriander, anise, rose or vanilla flavoring

pastry flour

Cream butter with a little flour, add molasses which has been boiled and cooled, with flavoring, and flour for stiff dough, about 2¼ qts. Mix as little as possible, cover and set in cold place for several hours. Shape into small thick cakes, or, roll about ½ in. thick, prick with fork or crease and cut into small cakes. Bake in moderate oven. Remove from tins as soon as baked.

With nice flavored molasses, no other flavoring is necessary. More shortening may be used.

## ★Molasses Snaps—no eggs

½ cup oil or butter, or half of each
1 cup sugar
2 cups flour
2 cups molasses
flavoring
more flour

Cream butter, sugar and the 2 cups of flour, pour hot molasses over, add flavoring and flour for stiff dough, perhaps about 6 cups; press together lightly, set in cold place for several hours; roll thin, bake in moderately quick oven and remove from tins at once. These cakes will be brittle when first made and will grow softer with time. One cup of butter may be used for richer cakes.

## Nut Wafers

1 cup chopped English walnut, pecan or hickory nut meats
1 cup dark brown sugar
2 eggs
4 level tablespns. flour
salt

Beat eggs, add sugar gradually, beating well; then add flour, salt and nuts. Mix, spread as thin as possible on buttered pans, set in cold place, bake in quick oven. When nearly cold, cut into squares.

## NutCakes—Bro. Hurdon

1 cup chopped nut meats

1 cup sugar

1 cup flour

1 egg

Mix, drop on well oiled tins some distance apart, bake. Remove from tins when taken from the oven.

## Hard Sponge Cakes

Cream together ¼ cup butter and 1 cup sugar, add 1 well beaten egg and 1 cup of flour to which has been added a pinch of salt; stir in 1 cup chopped nut meats; drop in spoonfuls on buttered tins and flatten or shape a little; bake in moderate oven.

## Risen Doughnuts—Baked

*Sponge—*

    1 cup milk

    ⅔ cake compressed yeast

    2 cups flour

Add dissolved yeast and flour to warm milk, beat well, let rise.

*When light—*

    ½ cup sugar

    5 tablespns. oil or melted butter

    vanilla, lemon, coriander or anise for flavoring

    2–2½ cups flour

    ¼ teaspn. salt

Beat oil and sugar together with a little flour, add flavoring, salt and light sponge, gradually, beating; then enough flour for a moderately stiff dough; knead a little and let rise. When well risen, roll ½ or ¾ in. thick, cut with doughnut cutter and place on floured, oiled tins some distance apart. Let rise, bake.

Roll in sugar with or without ground coriander seed or chopped nuts before laying on tins, if desired, or moisten with sugar syrup or white of egg and water and roll in sugar after baking.

Another half-spoon of oil may be added to sponge, with 1 white and 2 yolks of eggs well beaten, but eggs are not necessary. If a yellow color is desired, use a little saffron. Mix softer when eggs are used.

**Risen Doughnuts**

*Sponge*—
    1 cup skimmed milk
    ⅔ cake compressed, or
    2 tablespns. soft yeast
    2 cups flour

*When light*—
    3 tablespns. oil or melted butter
    ½ cup sugar
    salt
    flavouring
    yolk of 1 egg or not
    flour for rather stiff dough

Proceed as in baked doughnuts, lay on floured board, cover; when very light, fry in cooking or olive oil, hot enough for the cakes to rise to the top almost instantly. Turn at once with a fork. ⅓ of a cup of oil may be used in the cakes and 1 whole well beaten egg.

Our grandmothers' twisted doughnuts are dear to all our hearts.

Sometimes roll the dough thin, cut with biscuit cutter and put a teaspoonful of some jelly or jam on one side, fold the other side over, having moistened the edges, press well together, fry when light, roll in sugar. Baked doughnuts may be prepared the same.

## Crullers

    ⅓–½ cup butter
    ⅓–½ cup sugar
    3 eggs (separate if desired)

flour for soft dough

Mix, chill, roll thin, cut in strips 3½ in. long and 2 in. wade; cut 2 slits in each piece and give each strip of dough a twist. Fry in oil or bake in oven. When to be fried, use the smaller quantity of butter and sugar.

Crullers may have 4 incisions made lengthwise to within ⅓ of an in. of each end. To fry, take up the second and fourth strips and let the others separate in the middle from those in the hand as you drop them into the hot oil. For baking, it is better to twist the strips.

### Fried Cakes

1 cup milk

2 eggs

¾ cup sugar

salt, flour

3 tablespns. oil or melted butter

Add sugar and yolks of eggs to cold milk, agitate with wire batter whip until full of bubbles, sprinkle flour in gradually, keeping up the agitating motion. When the batter is quite stiff, beat in the oil gradually, and chop in the stiffly-beaten whites of eggs. Add flour for rather stiff dough and set in cold place for 2 hrs. or longer. Shape and fry the same as risen doughnuts.

## ICINGS AND FILLINGS FOR CAKES

Starch, which is changed into sugar in the process of digestion, and cane sugar, form so large a part of all cakes as to furnish in themselves an excess of that element; so why should we put a coating of almost solid sugar over the outside? Certainly not for hygienic reasons. If a cake is well baked, the icing only hides its beauty, and the excessive sweetness destroys the flavors of the finest cake. Let us not use it. Protest and recipes are both given.

Instead of icing, sometimes sift granulated, brown or powdered sugar over the top of the loaf of cake, or over one layer to be used for the top, before baking.

Glaze the top of molasses cookies or cakes before baking with a mixture of 1 yolk of egg and 2 tablespns. of milk.

Sprinkle half a cup of chopped or ground blanched almonds or other nuts over the top of the cake just before it goes into the oven, and cover the cake until nearly done to prevent browning the nuts.

The tops of cakes may be brushed after baking with equal parts of molasses and milk mixed.

## Water Icing

The simplest of icings is granulated, powdered or xxxx confectioner's sugar formed into a paste so that it will run just smooth, by the addition of hot or cold water. That made from granulated sugar must be made with hot water and be pretty stiff. It takes longer to dry and is more likely to run; that from powdered sugar is also quite likely to run. The icing made from confectioner's sugar is the most satisfactory. It is usually made with cold water, but one authority recommends hot water very positively.

One recipe for granulated sugar frosting is—

1 cup sugar, 1 tablespn. boiling water, beat until it will spread.

## Fruit Juice Icing

Stir rolled and sifted confectioner's sugar into any desired fruit juice until of the right consistency to spread; use a knife dipped in cold water to smooth the icing; 1–1½ tablespn. of liquid will be enough for the top of a medium sized loaf of cake.

If you have never made such an icing, you will be surprised to see how much sugar a little liquid will take. More icing is quickly made if you do not have enough.

When juices of different fruits are used in their season, the top of the cake may be decorated with the fruit whole, in halves or in slices. For instance, slices from the heart of strawberries, or, halves of red raspberries. The fruit may also be placed between the layers of the cake.

### Cream Icing

Stir confectioner's sugar into cream, plain or whipped, for both filling and icing.

If you have a little of these icings left over, cover it and set in a cold place, and add more liquid and sugar to it the next time.

### White of Egg Icing—Miss Stokes

white of 1 egg
1 tablespn. ice water
speck of salt
1 cup confectioner's sugar
flavoring

Beat white of egg with water, flavoring and salt to a stiff dry froth; add sugar until of the right consistency to spread, if too stiff, add quickly 1 teaspn. of cream or a few drops of water.

The icing is sometimes made by mixing the water and egg without beating and stirring the sugar in, making a smoother and more tender frosting. May use powdered sugar.

### White of Egg Icing with Lemon Juice

white of 1 egg
1 cup powdered sugar
1 tablespn. lemon juice
½ teaspn. vanilla

Put the white of egg into a bowl and add the sugar by degrees, beating; when the sugar is all in, add lemon juice and vanilla.

### Golden Icing

Yolks of 2 or 3 eggs and powdered sugar to make stiff enough to spread, about 1 cupful for 3 yolks; vanilla or orange flavoring or both. Beat until thick and creamy.

For an orange cake, use the juice and grated rind of a small orange to 3 yolks with the powdered sugar, and use for filling and icing. Sections of orange may be laid on top. Confectioner's sugar may be used.

### ★ Butter Frosting—almost like whipped cream

Work together 1 cup confectioner's sugar and 1 level tablespn. of butter. Flavor with vanilla. Add 1¼–1½ tablespn. of milk. Beat well.

### Jelly Icing

Beat a glass of jelly, a little at a time, into the whites of 2 eggs. If the jelly is very tart, use 2–3 tablespns. powdered sugar. Prepare the icing some little time before it is to be used and set on ice. Elder-berry jelly gives a delightful flavor and beautiful color. Quince is also nice.

## Boiled Icing

1 cup granulated sugar
⅓ cup water
white of 1 egg
½ teaspn. vanilla, or the proper proportion of any desired flavoring

Stir sugar and water together over the fire until sugar is dissolved, then boil without stirring until the syrup will spin in threads when dropped from the tines of a fork, or until a hard ball is formed when dropped into cold water. Pour slowly over the stiffly-beaten white of egg, beating briskly, until stiff enough to spread. If the icing gets too stiff, set over hot water or thin with a trifle of lemon or other fruit juice, or hot water. ½–1 teaspn. of lemon juice added to the white of egg when about half beaten will make the icing more creamy. Some beat the white of egg slightly, only.

2 or 3 whites may be used with this quantity of syrup. One writes that she turns her syrup on to a platter and allows it to become perfectly cold before beating in the eggs, and she thinks it is much smoother and nicer.

One combination of flavors is, ¼ teaspn. each vanilla, orange and strawberry, or 1 or 2 drops of rose in place of strawberry.

Bro. Cornforth's directions are excellent: "Boil the sugar and water till it threads well, not just till it begins to thread; then set the dish off the stove and cover tight while you beat the whites stiff; then pour the hot syrup in a small stream into the whites, beating continuously; beat till it becomes cool enough to spread on the cake."

### Boiled Milk Icing—no egg

1 cup granulated sugar
4 tablespns. milk, with or
without a little butter
or 1½ cup sugar and ½ cup milk

Boil 5 m., or until syrup stiffens in cold water; stir until thick enough to spread.

### Caramel Icing—no egg

1½ cup brown sugar, ½ cup cream. Boil until syrup stiffens when dropped in water. Substitute ⅔ cup sour cream for sweet, with brown or granulated sugar.

### Boiled Maple Icing—no egg

Add ¾ cup sweet cream to 2 cups rolled or grated maple sugar. Boil slowly until mixture will thread. Cool about half, stir in ½ cup chopped English walnut meats, beat until creamy, and spread over cake.

Half granulated sugar may be used, and ½ cup of milk with a little butter substituted for the cream.

### Maple Syrup Icing and Filling

Boil ¾–1 cup of maple syrup until it will form a soft ball in cold water. Pour over beaten white of egg. Beat until stiff enough to spread. If desired, stir in ½ cup of rolled butternut meats just before spreading on the cake. The syrup may be boiled until it threads.

## Whipped Cream

Flavored with vanilla is delightful, of course, on the top of thin loaves of cake cut in squares. Or, for filling, with chopped, blanched almonds, dry, fine-cut stewed prunes, or slices of banana.

Molasses cake baked in layers, with whipped cream between the layers and over the top, with or without a sprinkling of grated cocoanut, is considered a great treat in some households.

## Cocoanut Cream

1 cup cream, whipped.
⅓ cup sugar
1½ cup fresh grated cocoanut

Two layers and on top of cake, with cocoanut sprinkled over top. Some additional flavoring if desired.

## Butternut Filling

1 cup sweet cream, ½–¾ cup sugar and 1 cup rolled butternut meats, mixed without whipping cream. Flavoring if desired.

## ★ Sour Cream Filling

Before I gave up cake I used to think this filling had no equal:

½ cup thick sour cream
½ cup sugar
1½ cup chopped blanched almonds
1 teaspn. vanilla

Whip cream (ice-cold), sugar and vanilla together until just thick, taking care not to whip too long as sour cream turns to butter more easily than sweet; add the almonds, spread quickly between layers of cake and roughly on top. The nuts may be sprinkled over the layers of cream instead of being mixed with it. The white of an egg beaten stiff with part of the sugar is sometimes added to the whipped cream. Shellbark, English walnut or rolled butternut meats may be substituted for almonds.

### Creamed Apple

White of 1 large egg, 1½ cup granulated, powdered or confectioner's sugar, 2 or 3 medium sized apples. Peel apples and grate on to unbeaten white of egg and sugar in large bowl; beat for 20 m.; or until light and creamy. Lemon, rose or strawberry may be used if flavoring is desired. Spread between layers and on top of cold cake. Bananas, peaches and other fruits rubbed through a fine colander may be used the same as apples.

Steamed quarters of apples may be used.

### Cocoanut Filling

Spread under and upper sides of layers of warm cake with soft icing. Sprinkle tops with fresh grated cocoanut and put other layers on. Use plenty of icing on top of last layer and sprinkle well with cocoanut.

### Date Filling

Stone and skin dates after boiling a moment, mash or grind them, and add water if necessary; spread between layers of cake. Cover the top of the cake with coffee icing with cream. Chopped nuts may be mixed with the dates and sprinkled over the top of the cake.

## Pineapple Filling and Icing

Chop fresh pineapple and sprinkle with sugar; drain after 3 or 4 hrs; add beaten whites of 2 eggs, ⅔ cup sugar and 1 teaspn. lemon juice to 1 cup of pineapple and place between layers. Use some of the juice with confectioner's sugar for icing the top and sides of the cake. When using confectioner's sugar with pineapple omit whites of eggs.

Drain canned pineapple very dry, chop and add lemon juice and confectioner's sugar, when fresh pineapple is not obtainable.

## Imperial Filling

Spread layers of cake with jelly and the following:

*Filling—*
    1 cup chopped raisins
    ½ cup chopped almonds
    ½ cup grated cocoanut
    white of 1 egg

Beat white stiff, add other ingredients and spread.

## Coffee Icing

Add confectioner's sugar and vanilla to strong cereal coffee, with or without a little heavy cream.

## Fig Jelly Filling

    1 lb. figs, chopped fine
    1 cup sugar

½ cup boiling water

Boil to a jelly, stirring constantly, or cook in double boiler until thick.

### Prune Filling

Stew ½ lb. of prunes in a very little water, rub through colander or cut fine, add whites of 2 eggs beaten to a stiff froth with 2 tablespns. of sugar.

### Nut and Raisin Filling

1½ cup sugar
½ cup water
white of 1 large or 2 small eggs
1 cup each of chopped or ground raisins and nut meats
1 teaspn. vanilla

Boil sugar and water till the syrup will form a soft ball in cold water; pour it into the stiffly-beaten white of egg, add nuts and raisins and spread while warm between the layers.

Raisins or nuts alone may be used. Shellbarks or butternuts are especially enjoyable. Figs or dates may be substituted for the raisins or for the nuts.

### ★ Cream Filling

1 cup milk
⅓–½ cup sugar
2¼ tablespns. (¼ cup) flour
1 egg or 2 yolks, or 1 egg and yolk of another
½ teaspn. vanilla

Mix sugar and flour dry, pour boiling milk over, boil up, turn over beaten eggs, stirring, return to fire and heat until creamy but do not boil; set dish at once into cold water, add flavoring.

Use ½ tablespn. less of flour for Washington Pie, and ¼ cream (or a small piece of butter) in the milk.

½ cup of flour is sometimes used. Add cocoanut for a cocoanut cake.

### Royal Filling and Icing

¼ cup milk
¼ cup orange juice
¼ cup flour
½ cup sugar
yolk of 1 egg
oil from rind of half an orange
6 drops vanilla
1 drop rose

Flavor sugar with oil of orange, make cream according to directions for cream filling and add rose and vanilla when partly cool. Icing of cream and confectioner's sugar, tinted with pink.

I have usually used this for Royal Sponge Cake and this quantity is sufficient for one large layer.

### Filling for Lemon Pie Cake and Washington Pie

¾–1 cup sugar
1½ tablespn. corn starch or 2 of flour
1 teaspn. butter
1 cup water

yolk 1 egg

3 tablespns. lemon juice

2–6 drops lemon extract or grated rind of ½ a lemon

salt

Mix sugar and corn starch or flour, drop the teaspoon of butter on and pour the boiling water over gradually, stirring; boil up well and add 2 or 3 tablespns. to the yolk of egg stirring; then add yolk to the mixture and cook like custard. Remove from fire and when partially cooled add flavoring. Use sometimes for the filling of a cake with whipped cream on the top.

## Lemon Cheese for Cakes

¼ cup butter

¾ cup sugar

2 whites and 3 yolks of egg

3 tablespns. lemon juice

grated rind of 1 lemon

Cook in double boiler, cool, spread between layers of sponge or other cake or on crisp pastry, or put it into cream puff shells; or, without cooking put into pastry in patty pans and bake in moderate oven.

## Marshmallow Filling

1 oz. (about 4 tablespns.) sifted powdered gum arabic, 4 tablespns. water, ½ cup sugar, whites 3 eggs, 1 teaspn. vanilla. Soak gum arabic in water for 1 hour, add sugar, cook in double boiler ½ hour, add stiffly-beaten whites of eggs and vanilla, beat until stiff and white.

Nice for 2 or 3-days old angel cake split in halves or thirds.

# ICE CREAM AND FRUIT ICES

Neither very hot nor very cold foods should be taken at meals. If foods are too hot, the stomach is debilitated, and if they are very cold, vitality must be drawn from the system to warm them before the work of digestion can be carried on; so it would be better to take ice cream and all ices by themselves rather than as a dessert.

When ices are served for dessert, they should be eaten very slowly.

Water ices, sherbets and frozen fruits, without large quantities of sugar, are invaluable in cases of fever.

I am not going into the subject of ice cream exhaustively for there are plenty of books on that subject already, but will give you my own recipe which must be tried to be appreciated.

The little flour in it gives it a smoothness and creaminess with one third to one half milk equal to all cream without it; and does not give the disagreeable flavor of corn starch; also, made by this method, the cream and milk are sterilized.

Try the cream without any flavoring and see how delicious it is.

Use wet snow instead of ice for freezing in the winter. It works even better and is less trouble.

Beat the cream well with a wooden spoon after removing the dasher.

Add fruit or nuts to cream when removing the dasher, so that they will not become hard as they would do if frozen with the cream.

For freezing, have the ingredients cold. Have the ice very fine; the finer it is, the better the results. One-third as much rock salt should be at hand. The ice and salt may be mixed, or may be put around the freezer in the proportion of 3 inches of ice to 1 inch of salt.

First, adjust the freezer, having the mixture to be frozen in the can. Fill not over ⅔ full to allow for expansion. Then pack with the ice and salt, turning the handle around once in a while during the operation, to keep the mixture from freezing to the sides of the can. Have a stick to pound the ice and salt down well around the can.

Turn slowly at first to make a fine grain, then more rapidly as the cream thickens.

Before removing the cover to take out the dasher, scrape away the ice and salt and wipe off the water on the lid and near the top of the can, so that none can possibly get into the cream. Beat the cream and replace the cover, with a clean cork in the top. Drain off a part of the water and repack the can, using less salt than at first, sometimes not any, so as not to have the cream too hard. To be at its best, cream should be stiff enough only to hold its shape. Cover with paper, a blanket or carpet and let stand to "ripen" for 2 hours or longer. This part is important, as the flavor and texture are perfected only by standing.

If possible, open the can in an hour and a half and stir the cream so that the soft center comes to the edge of the can. Repack and cover the same and let stand for 2 or 3 hours.

Save the salt from the bottom of the freezer to use another time, and it is a good plan to save a little of the thick salt water to use instead of the last layer of salt near the top of the can for the next freezing, as it facilitates the work very much.

In serving, dip the spoon into hot water each time before putting it into the cream; this, with care, will give a nice shaped serving.

Pop corn without butter or salt is more suitable to serve with ice cream than cake.

Sugar syrup gives a finer, smoother and more substantial grain to frozen fruits, sherbets and water ices than sugar and water, and they do not melt as quickly when exposed to the air.

Pack all ices the same as creams and let stand the same after freezing, to become smooth and mellow.

For water ices, do not turn the crank continuously. Turn slowly and rest between, until the ice becomes quite stiff. This is the rule, but for a change the freezer may be turned rapidly and continuously, with a different result.

Stir sherbets constantly. Serve both sherbets and water ices in glasses.

Vegetable gelatine is an improvement to ices, giving body to them.

There is a great difference in freezers. Be sure to get a good one. The construction of the dasher has much to do with the texture of the cream. Those that freeze the quickest are not necessarily the best.

Do not buy a small freezer: you can freeze a small quantity in a large freezer, but you cannot freeze a large quantity in a small freezer.

## ★ The "Laurel" Ice Cream

2½ pts. heavy cream
2½ pts. whole milk
2 cups sugar
4 or 5 tablespns. pastry flour

Stir the flour smooth with some of the cold milk and heat the remainder of the milk, with the cream and sugar, in a double boiler and when hot, set over the fire. Let it boil up quickly, stir in the flour and when boiling all through, return to the double boiler for a few minutes, beating well. Or, heat the milk and cream only in the double boiler and pour gradually, stirring, over the sugar and flour which have been mixed together. Return to boiler and cook for 10–15 m. Turn through a fine wire strainer into a large pan to cool quickly; stir while cooling.

Do not take too large measures of flour.

Any kind of cream may be made from this. Flavor with vanilla for vanilla cream, or tint pink and flavor with ¾–1 teaspn. of strawberry extract for strawberry cream, or with a few drops of rose, for rose cream. Tint green and flavor with almond and vanilla for pistachio cream, using only a few drops of almond to a teaspn. of vanilla. This may have a few shredded almonds stirred into the frozen cream.

Sometimes sprinkle fresh grated cocoanut over each serving of cream, or the cocoanut may be stirred in as other flavorings are.

A very pretty cream is one with citron and candied cherries cut into tiny pieces and added when the dasher is removed.

We make a fruit and nut cream which is liked very much, by adding well washed English currants, raisins cut in quarters, citron in small pieces and coarse chopped English walnuts or pecans. Omit the nuts for a fruit cream.

For coffee cream, steep (not boil) cereal coffee in milk for 10 to 20 m. Strain through a cloth and use as plain milk with the cream. Flavor with vanilla.

One quart of sweetened, crushed strawberries or raspberries added to the recipe makes the right proportion for fruit cream. Drained, finely-shredded or grated pineapple makes a general favorite in cream.

## Maple Ice Cream

1 qt. genuine maple syrup
1 qt. heavy cream
1 qt. light cream

¾ qt. milk

7 tablespns. flour

## Lemon Ice

8–12 tablespns. lemon juice

1 orange

2½ cups sugar

1 qt. water including the gelatine

⅛ oz. vegetable gelatine

Soak and cook gelatine according to directions (p. 335), add water to make 1 cup, keep warm; cook sugar and 3 cups of water together for 5 minutes and strain into the gelatine. Prepare the lemon and orange juice, and if desired, shave off a little of the thin yellow rind and let it stand in the juice for a few minutes, then strain it out. When the gelatine mixture is partially cooled, add the juice gradually, stirring. The orange may be omitted.

Or, omit gelatine, boil sugar with 1 qt. of water and when cool combine with the juice.

## Orange Ice

1 pt. sugar

1 qt. water

1 pt. of orange juice

6–8 tablespns. lemon juice

⅛ oz. vegetable gelatine

Flavor juice with thin yellow rind of orange and proceed as in lemon ice, omitting gelatine if preferred.

### Raspberry Ice

1 cup raspberry juice

¾ cup sugar (less if juice is already sweetened)

1 pt. water

2 tablespns. lemon juice

1 sixteenth oz. vegetable gelatine, or not

Cook sugar and water together and add to prepared gelatine. When nearly cool, add raspberry juice and stir occasionally until cool. Freeze.

### Currant and Raspberry Ice

2 cups currant juice

1 cup raspberry juice

1 pt. water

1–1½ cup sugar

⅛ oz. gelatine, or not

Proceed as in Raspberry Ice.

Use cherry, strawberry, quince, gooseberry, grape or pineapple for ices, varying the proportion of sugar and water according to the sweetness of the fruit. Pineapples should be grated and with the lemon juice added to cold syrup and strained through a sieve. Pineapple is one of the most delightful ices.

### Mint Ice

Add fine cut or chopped spearmint to lemon ice mixture just before freezing, or to orange ice for orange mint ice.

## ★ Grape Sherbet

1½–1¾ cup sugar
1 qt. water, scant
scant ¼ oz. vegetable gelatine
5–6 tablespns. lemon juice
2 cups grape juice
whites of 2 eggs
2 tablespns. powdered sugar

Flavor the sugar with oil of lemon if desired, and boil with the water for 5 m. only. Prepare the gelatine with a scant cup of water, and add to warm syrup; cool; add lemon and grape juice, stirring. Put into freezer and stir for 15 m. Beat the whites of eggs until light but not stiff; add the powdered sugar and beat 2 m., add to the sherbet in the freezer and finish freezing. Ripen from 2 to 4 hours. This sherbet is of a beautiful lavender color when finished.

Substitute other fruit juices for the grape, varying the quantity of sugar. Red raspberry is better in water ice, as the whites of the eggs spoil its flavor.

## ★ Mint Sherbet

1 qt. water
1½ cup sugar
5–7 good-sized stalks of mint
⅓–½ cup lemon juice
white of 1 large or 2 small eggs

1½ tablespn. powdered sugar

scant ¼ oz. vegetable gelatine

scant cup of water

Boil sugar and water and add to gelatine prepared with the scant cup of water. When cool, add stirring, the lemon juice and fine cut or chopped mint. Stir in freezer 15 m. Add whites of eggs beaten with powdered sugar as in grape sherbet and finish freezing. Ripen.

### Pineapple Sherbet, or Frozen Pineapple

1¾ pint fine ground pineapple

large 2½ cups sugar

1 qt. liquid, gelatine and all

¼ oz. gelatine

1½–2 tablespns. lemon juice

whites of 2 eggs

2 tablespns. powdered sugar

Shred and grind nice, ripe pineapples. Prepare gelatine with 1 cup of water and add more to make 1½ cup. Cook sugar and 2½ cups of water together for 5 m. and add to gelatine. When nearly cool, combine with pineapple and lemon juice; cool; stir in freezer for 15 m. Add whites of eggs beaten with powdered sugar and finish freezing. Ripen.

### Mina's Lemon and Orange Sherbets

*Lemon—*

    4 lemons

    4 oranges

1 lb. sugar

1 qt. water

whites of 4, or less, eggs

⅛ oz. of vegetable gelatine

*Orange—*

10 oranges

1 lemon

1 pt. sugar

1 qt. water

whites of 4, or less, eggs

⅛ oz. vegetable gelatine

Follow directions for Grape Sherbet.

## Frozen Strawberries

1 qt. berries

2 cups sugar

3 or 4 tablespns. lemon juice

1 qt. water

Add 1 cup of sugar and the lemon juice to well mashed berries. Let stand in ice box 1–2 hours. Boil water and remaining sugar together for 5 m., cool, add to berry mixture, freeze, ripen. Serve plain or with whipped cream.

## Frozen Peaches

1 qt., in pieces, of nice ripe peaches

1–1½ cup sugar

1 qt. water

1–2 cups cream

Rub measured peaches through colander; add cold syrup made by boiling sugar and water together for 10 m. Freeze. Stir in cream whipped and slightly sweetened, when dasher is removed. Repack and ripen.

## Frappés

Frappés are partly frozen mixtures of fruit juices, pulps or fine grated fruits and when not too sweet are excellent in fevers and are often served in place of a drink or a sherbet to well people. Of course they are served in glasses.

# CEREALS

"The grains, with fruits, nuts and vegetables contain all the nutritive properties necessary to make good blood."

"Those who eat flesh are eating grains and vegetables at second-hand; for the animal receives from these things the nutrition that produces growth."

"The life that was in the grains and vegetables passes into the eater. We receive it by eating the flesh of the animal. How much better to get it direct, by eating the food that God provided for our use."

"Grains used for porridge or mush should have several hours' cooking; but soft or liquid foods are less wholesome than dry foods which require thorough mastication."

When porridges are used, something dry like zwieback or crisp crackers should be eaten with them to induce mastication.

Foods containing starch should be well insalivated by thorough mastication before any tart foods are introduced into the stomach, as acid hinders the digestion of starch.

The large proportion of starch contained in grains is changed to sugar in the process of digestion, so the addition of more sugar gives an excess of that element, overtaxing the liver and increasing the tendency to fermentation, since both starch and sugar are substances that ferment easily. Then if milk, another easily fermented food, is added what can be said of the combination? Besides: "the presence of a considerable amount of sugar actually retards the digestion of starch."—*Dr. Kress.*

For those who feel that they cannot at once forego the sweet, stir in a few sliced dates to graham porridge or sprinkle them over the top and serve with nut or dairy cream. Chopped figs or stewed raisins may also be used the same with different cereals. A very harmonious combination is pearled barley cooked with raisins. Nice ripe blueberries or black raspberries may be served with cereals.

A complete meal may be made of graham or any preferred porridge, blanched almonds, English walnuts or pecans, with dates, figs or raisins. The combination will be satisfying without any milk or cream.

My readers will many of them be surprised to find that oatmeal and some other porridges are delightful served with cream sauce, old-fashioned milk gravy, macaroni sauce and other gravies; the cooked parched grains especially so. A poached egg may be placed on each serving of porridge, with or without sauce.

Raw rice may be ground coarse or fine for different purposes.

The parched grains may be served with suitable, sub-acid fruits.

The toasted breakfast cereals on the market, prepared without malt or any additional sweet are many of them excellent foods because of the dextrinization of the starch, and we can easily prepare dextrinized grains in our own homes.

### Parched Sweet Corn—the Ideal Cereal Preparation

Put dried sweet corn into a corn popper, iron frying pan or round bottomed iron kettle; cover, and shake over the fire until the grains are browned and puffed up nearly round. Served plain, this corn supplies a complete and satisfying food, as any one will find who sits down with a nice fresh-parched porridge dish of it and chews it until it is fine and creamy in the mouth. It is much more delicious than the finest popcorn. It may be ground and eaten in cold or hot milk, nut or dairy, and it may have a little salt and sterilized butter mixed with it while it is warm. A cup of cereal coffee or tea-hygiene with a dish of parched corn makes a nice luncheon or supper.

The corn may be dried on the cob or shelled and dried. It may often be bought from dealers in seeds, after the planting season is over.

Parched field corn is a good nourishing food but not so sweet and tender. It is usually better to be ground.

One doctor says, "I could travel the world around on parched corn and never want grease of any kind."

It is well understood that corn and oatmeal are the richest in oil of any of the grains. In some countries the soldiers carry parched corn in their pockets on long marches.

### Yolk—Egg

Put yellow corn meal into an iron kettle or saucepan over a moderate fire; stir until of an even rich brown color. Serve warm or cold with hot or cold milk or cream. The donor of this recipe says: "When I was a child this was considered a great dainty, but I do not know how it obtained its name or where we learned to make it."

The different preparations of grains may all be parched the same as sweet corn and corn meal in the preceding recipes. If more convenient they may be done in the oven but the flavor is not as good. Some of them are tender enough to be eaten dry or in milk without any further preparation; others are better to be ground before adding the milk or cream, and some need to stand in the milk, hot or cold, for a time, before serving, while others (rice especially) require cooking after parching. Some are better cooked in milk.

### Pop-corn

To pop: "Wet the corn slightly and let it dry on the stove; put it in the popper while it is hot and in four minutes every kernel should be turned inside out, crisp and tender."—*From a clipping.*

Serve the popped kernels plain with nuts, cereal coffee, tea-hygiene, cream or milk, or sprinkle delicately with salt and turn a little oil or melted butter over, mixing thoroughly.

Put together the poorly popped kernels of corn and all the remains, cover with cold water and soak until soft, perhaps over night. Then add milk and cook in a double boiler ½ hour or so. Serve with cream or more milk if necessary, or, cook in all water and serve with cream. These leftovers may be ground and soaked in milk until soft.

## Rusk

Dry slices or pieces of bread in the oven and brown delicately, grind through the food cutter and serve in milk or with cream.

## Porridges

"Some people degrade these foods by calling them mushes, a horrible name, by the way; the good English word porridge is much better, and porridge is not gruel."—*An Editor.*

Unless cereals are steamed, they should be cooked in a double boiler or something that answers the same purpose.

A flat or round wire batter whip is the best for stirring the grain into the water, as that keeps even the finest flour from becoming lumpy.

The very most important thing in making porridges is to have the liquid boiling when the cereal is put in. If it stops boiling while the grain is being added there will be a raw taste to the porridge, no matter how long it cooks.

Put the required amount of water, with the salt, 1 teaspn. to a quart of water, into the inner cup of a double boiler. Heat the water to bubbling boiling, sprinkle the measured grain in so slowly as not to stop the boiling of the water, stirring continuously. Let it boil up well, and if a coarse grain, cook over the fire until it thickens, then set into the outer boiler containing perfectly boiling water and keep it cooking rapidly the required length of time.

Do not stir after the grain thickens. Watch that the outer boiler does not become dry. Grains for breakfast may be cooked while you have a fire the day before, then all that is necessary in the morning is to set the inner boiler into the outer one containing boiling water and heat it through. If there should be water standing on top of the porridge, pour it off before heating, but under no circumstances stir the porridge, or add any more water while heating, or a pasty, tasteless dish will be the result.

When the porridge is to be re-heated, a slightly larger proportion of water should be used, and for steaming, a smaller quantity.

One advantage in steaming is that the cereal (after being started over the fire in some suitable utensil) can be turned into an earthen dish and set into the steamer, warmed in the morning and sent to the table in the same dish.

Farina, cream of wheat and similar cereals are more palatable and nourishing if cooked in part milk. These finer preparations may have milk or cream stirred into them just before serving.

## Proportion of Water and Length of Time for Cooking Different Cereals

|  |  | |  |
|---|---|---|---|
| Graham Flour | 1 part to 2 or 3 | of water | cook 1–2 hrs. |
| Rolled Wheat | 1 part to 2 or 3 | of water | cook 3–4 hrs. |
| Cracked Wheat | 1 part to 4½ or 5 | of water | cook 4–6 hrs. |
| Pearled Wheat | 1 part to 4 or 4½ | of water | cook 4–6 hrs. |
| Whole Wheat | 1 part to 6 | of water | cook 6–8 hrs. |

| | | | |
|---|---|---|---|
| Rolled Oats | 1 part to 2 or 3 | of water | cook 3–4 hrs. |
| Oatmeal | 1 part to 4 or 4½ | of water | cook 4–6 hrs. |
| Pearled Barley | 1 part to 5 | of water | cook 4–5 hrs. |
| Hominy, coarse | 1 part to 5 | of water | cook 6–8 hrs. |
| Hominy, fine | 1 part to 4 or 5 | of water | cook 4–6 hrs. |
| Corn Meal | 1 part to 3 or 5 | of water | cook 2–5 hrs. |
| Rice | 1 part to 3 or 4 | of water | 25 m–1¼ hr. |
| Farina | 5 tablespns. to 1 qt. | liquid | 1 hr. |

Different lots of graham flour and rolled oats vary, so that it is not possible to make an exact rule for them, but graham flour should be stirred into water until the mixture is quite stiff because it grows thinner by cooking.

Rye meal makes one of the most delightful porridges. Stir the meal slowly into boiling salted water, the same as graham flour, and cook for 1 hour at least.

Whole wheat is a very satisfying and inexpensive food. Some families buy it by the bushel and use large quantities of it in different ways. Some put the boiled wheat into bread sponge before mixing it up.

Different kinds of corn meal vary, too. Only about ⅔ or ¾ as much granular meal is required for a given amount of liquid as of other kinds.

Oatmeal is difficult of digestion, is apt to cause fermentation and should be partaken of sparingly even when well cooked, except by those of strong digestive powers. One young man said in my presence, "I never know I have a stomach except when I eat oatmeal."

Cracked wheat is very nice cooked with an extra quantity of water, molded and served cold.

With a Vegetarian Society mill delightful cracked wheat and many other cereal foods can be made.

Cracked corn—samp grits—hominy, is a valuable food. Besides the package preparations I have bought it at feed stores in the East and obtained it from the mills in the West, and with a mill it can be made at home. It should be thoroughly cooked. The old-fashioned way is to put it into a round bottomed iron kettle with salt and plenty of water (adding more water when necessary) and cook it all day. It may be served with milk, butter or gravy, or with any of the sauces used for macaroni, and may be cooked with tomato and onion the same as pilau, p. 131.

## RICE

"Rice is the most easily digested of all the cereals. The Japanese, famous for their athletic superiority and wonderful endurance, use rice unpolished. The rice of commerce is not only stripped of much of its most desirable qualities, but in order to make it attractive it is coated with glucose and talc to produce the pearly appearance. Persons using such rice should be careful to wash it thoroughly. After once eating unpolished rice, the rice of commerce will never again be accepted. To eat polished rice is like eating shavings instead of real, satisfying substance."—*Henry S. Clubb, President Vegetarian Society of America, in "Life and Health," and "The Vegetarian."*

Wash commercial rice in several waters, scrubbing it thoroughly with the hands, in a colander set in a pan of water, rinsing the colander up and down. Then put it over the fire in cold water, boil for 5 m. and drain, before cooking after any of the methods.

### To Boil Rice

After washing and parboiling rice, throw it into 3 or 4 times its bulk of boiling salted water, stir it over a hot fire until it rolls up in the rapidly boiling water. Let it boil in this way until it swells, then set into the outer boiler or on the back of the stove on a pad until it is perfectly tender. If rice is cooked in a double boiler, use the smaller quantity of water, and the larger if cooked altogether over the fire. Do not stir after it begins to swell. This is practically the Japanese method.

Another Japanese way is to soak the rice over night, drain and put to cooking in an equal quantity of boiling water, keeping closely covered all of the time.

## Chinese Way of Cooking Rice

After washing, put rice over the fire in double its bulk of cold water, let it boil up well, carefully lift cover to see if water is all absorbed; if not, drain, sprinkle salt over if desired (the Chinaman does not use it), return to fire closely covered and watch, listening until a faint crackling of parching grains at the bottom is heard; then remove to the back of the range where the rice will just steam—"steam fragrant." When ready to serve, carefully stir the grain with a wooden skewer or some small round stick, when the snowy mass should crumble apart into indistinct kernels. "Try the Chinaman's way and be convinced that plain boiled rice is a palatable, substantial food."—*Adapted from Mrs. J. N. Anderson, Canton, China, in "Life and Health."*

## The Indian Way

Wash the rice, put little by little into 8 times its bulk (2 qts. to a cup) of rapidly boiling salted water. Stir occasionally at first with a fork until the rice is rolling up continuously from the rapid boiling. Cook until tender, 15–25 m., according to the age and quality of the rice. Be sure to cook it until it is tender but not a moment longer. Drain in a fine colander, pour cold water over to separate the kernels, put into the dish in which it is to be served and set in a steamer or in the edge of the oven for a half hour. The water drained from the rice may be used for soup.

### To Steam Rice

After washing, soak 1 cup of rice in 1¼ cup of warm water for an hour or longer, in a dish suitable for serving it in. Add 1 level teaspn. of salt and 1 cup of milk and steam, without stirring, for just 1 hour. Serve at once, or if it has to stand, cover close so that the top kernels will not become hard.

All milk may be used by taking 2¾–3 cups. If the milk fills the dish so that it is just ready to run over, the rice when steamed will stand snowy white above the top of the dish.

### ★ Baked Rice

A nice supper or luncheon dish or dessert.

½–¾ cup rice
½ teaspn. salt
2 qts. rich milk

Parboil rice 5 m. and drain, add it to milk in pudding dish, stir even in bottom of dish, set in slow oven, cover and bake 2–3 hrs. without stirring, or until milk is all thickened and creamy with rice; if the milk boils over under the cover, the oven is too hot. This is so delicious that it does not require anything additional in eating but it may be served with sugar, maple sugar or syrup.

### Parched Rice

Wash if commercial rice, spread on tin and put in warm place to dry. When thoroughly dried, put in slow oven and color to an even light brown. Soak for 1 hour in an equal quantity of lukewarm water, then add 3 times the quantity of rich milk, with or without 1 level teaspn. salt to the cup of rice; steam, or cook in double boiler for 1 hour. Serve plain. The rice may be ground.

### Granella—to Serve

Pour just enough hot water over granella to moisten it a trifle. Mix lightly and serve with cream. Granella is nice in hot milk.

### Baked Hominy

1 cup cold, fine hominy porridge
1 teaspn. butter

1 teaspn. sugar

1 pt. milk

salt

3 eggs

Mix hominy and yolks of eggs thoroughly; add melted butter, then sugar and salt and the milk gradually, mixing hominy to smooth paste. Chop in stiffly-beaten whites and bake in buttered dish in moderate oven. Serve as vegetable for dinner or as principal dish for luncheon or supper.

### To Hull Corn

2 gallons cold water, 1 tablespn. concentrated lye or potash, 4 qts. corn, white corn if possible. Dissolve lye in water, add corn, and boil (adding water to keep covered) until the hulls will rub off. Wash and rub in several clear waters until the hulls are all off. Soak over night or for several hours in cold water; drain and put to cooking in boiling water. Cook until tender, all day if necessary. Add salt a little while before it is done, then cook until as dry as possible without scorching. Serve as a vegetable, plain, or with cream or cream sauce. Eat in milk or with nut meats.

The hulled corn may be dried. Hard wood ashes may be used to make the lye for cooking the corn, or a bag containing 2 cups of ashes may be boiled in the kettle with the corn. By boiling for 4 hrs., the hulls may be removed by using 1 tablespn. of soda to each 4 qts. of corn. Some prefer strong lime water for hulling.

Instead of soaking over night, the corn may be parboiled in 2 waters before cooking.

### ★ Granella No. 1—wheat, corn and oats

½ lb. (2 cups) bread flour
1 oz. (scant ½ cup) rolled oats
½ oz. (1½ tablespn.) common yellow corn meal
trifle salt
about ⅝ cup cold water

Mix dry ingredients and to ¾ of the quantity add water for a stiff dough, then work in the remaining ¼ until almost too stiff to knead; roll and pound out to ¼ or ⅓ inch thick, cut in round or square biscuit and set in cold place for 2 hours or more. Bake in a slow oven until a rich cream color or golden brown all through. Then grind coarse or fine as desired.

When oat *flour* is used, ⅓ of a cup only will be required.

It will take 2 tablespns. of Rhode Island meal to make ½ oz. and 1 only of yellow granular meal. The granular meal will need to be scalded with a part of the water or it will feel sandy in the granella.

The weights for a larger quantity are:

8½ lbs. bread flour, 1 lb. oats, ½ lb. corn meal, 1½ oz. salt.

### Granella No. 2—rice, wheat and barley

¼ cup rice
2¼ cups bread flour
¾ cup barley grits
salt
water

Cook rice in one cup water, cool, add salt, flour and grits, knead to very stiff dough, adding a trifle more water if necessary. Finish as No. 1.

½ cup rice *flour*, 1½ cup bread flour and ¾ cup barley grits may be used instead of the above combination.

### Granella No. 3—rye, wheat and barley

½ cup rye meal

2 cups bread flour

1 cup barley grits

salt

### Granella No. 4—rye, wheat and corn

½ cup rye meal

2 cups bread flour

1–2 tablespns. corn meal

salt

water

# MACARONI (ITALIAN PASTE)

Macaroni is one of the most important of cereal foods. The best—Italian—is made from a wheat rich in gluten, so to a great extent it supplies the place of meat.

One of the first things we do when we go into a new place is to hunt up an Italian macaroni store, as that is the only place where the genuine article is to be found. That made in this country, put up with a foreign label on the package, is inferior.

The Italian pastes come in a great variety of shapes and are named according to the shape. Macaroni, spaghetti and vermicelli are well known; then there are lasagne (broad and flat), rigatoni (large corrugated), da natali, ditali rigati, cannaroni rigati and reginnetti with mostacioli bianchi, soprafini (fine vermicelli), ditalini and acini di pepe—a few of the many. There are some small fine pastes put up in dainty boxes, especially for invalids, that are very delicate and digestible.

Those who have visited macaroni factories in Italy where macaroni is made for exportation, say that everything in connection with the food is neat and clean and that the macaroni is dried in closed rooms entirely removed from the dust of the street. That which travellers see drying by the roadside, exposed to the dust, is from small or private factories for home consumption.

## To Cook Macaroni

Do not wash or soak it. Break it when necessary and put into perfectly boiling salted water, 8 parts water to 1 of macaroni. Stir as soon as it is put into the water and often, until it begins to roll up, from the rapid boiling. Keep over a hot fire where it will continue to roll in boiling until well swollen and nearly done, then set back to simmer slowly. When perfectly tender (which will be in from ½ to 1 hour according to the size, age and quality, the better quality taking longer) turn into a colander and when drained, turn cold water over it, or, let it stand in cold water until ready to use.

Vermicelli and the other small varieties for soup require only twice their bulk of water, and some of them require 10 m. only for cooking. They will usually just absorb the water.

When preferred, macaroni may be cooked in just the amount of liquid it will absorb, which will be about 4 times its bulk. It may be cooked sometimes in a rich consommé, sometimes in milk in a double boiler, or in milk and water. It is often partly cooked in water, drained and finished in milk.

The "traditional" way of cooking spaghetti is to put the ends into water and coil it around in the kettle as it softens, cooking in full lengths and eating it the same, but the propriety of this method is questionable. In the first place, its sauce is apt to spatter in the effort to introduce the coil into the mouth, and mastication is sure to be incomplete.

The measurements of macaroni vary according to the size. For a large open variety, a cup and a half will be required where it would take only a cup of a small kind, or of the ordinary pipe-stem macaroni broken into inch lengths.

There is nothing that gives such character to macaroni as to cook a little garlic with it, a very little for some tastes, not more than ½ a clove to each cupful, less even, if the macaroni is not to be drained and the cloves are large. We seldom cook any preparation of macaroni without it, and people wonder why our macaroni has such a good taste. Not enough should be used to give a positive garlic flavor.

Pine nuts and sour cream give the cheese flavor. A good quality of macaroni is good without any sauce, just cooked in salted water and eaten slowly with nuts; but it may be served with any desired, tasty sauce. The mushroom sauces, Italian or Boundary Castle are especially delightful with it, but many others are excellent, olive and nut butter, old-fashioned milk gravy, lentil gravy, a good cream sauce, cream of tomato sauce, or any of the nice, meaty flavored sauces, or parsley butter.

Sometimes return macaroni to the fire after draining, and add a little butter, with or without chopped parsley, for those who use butter, or a little milk and butter or a few spoonfuls of cream. Then another time, put this cream or butter macaroni into a vegetable dish and pour a few hot stewed tomatoes over it.

### Baked Macaroni in Cream Sauce

1–1½ cup macaroni, according to size
2 small onions
1–2 small cloves of garlic
1 qt. water
1½–2 teaspns. salt

*Sauce*:—

1½ tablespn. oil
1½ tablespn. flour
1 large pt. milk
salt, crumbs
chopped parsley

Make cream sauce in the usual way with the oil, flour, salt and milk and pour into baking dish, turn into it the macaroni which has been cooked in the salted water with sliced onion and garlic until tender and the water absorbed, and press down into the sauce; sprinkle with crumbs and parsley and bake in moderate oven until bubbling and delicately browned. If preferred, ¼ cup of flour may be used in the sauce.

Make enough of this dish for two days, and another day stir salted tomato into what is left and bake as before for Macaroni in Tomato Sauce.

### Macaroni—Pine Nuts

Add ½ cup of pine nut butter or meal to the sauce in the preceding recipe (by mixing a little of the sauce with it) and sprinkle with chopped meats and crumbs.

### Macaroni—Corn

¾–1 cup macaroni
3 cups boiling water
1–1½ teaspn. salt
1 small onion
½–1 small clove of garlic if wished
1 cup canned, or stewed fresh corn

*Sauce:—*

1 cup rich milk or thin cream
½ tablespn. flour
½ teaspn. salt

Add corn and cooked macaroni to sauce, turn all into baking dish, sprinkle with crumbs and pour a little melted butter over if sauce is made with milk. Brown in oven.

### Browned Macaroni and Granella

1 cup macaroni, ¾–1 cup granella, 3 cups rich milk (more if necessary). Dry and delicately brown macaroni in oven and cook the same as unbrowned. Put into baking dish in layers with granella, turn milk, slightly salted, over and heat in moderate oven. It should be quite moist when done. Unless the milk is about one-fourth cream, there may be a little oil or butter poured over the top.

### Macaroni—Tomato and Onion

Simmer onion in oil or butter, add stewed tomatoes and salt; simmer a few minutes and add cooked macaroni; set back where it will heat slowly for a short time and serve.

Tomatoes, onions and macaroni may be put into baking dish in layers, with a sprinkling of pine nut meal; with tomatoes, crumbs and chopped nuts on top, and baked.

### Vermicelli—Asparagus

Cook vermicelli in salted water, drain, spread on platter, lay stalks of cooked asparagus on it and pour egg cream sauce over. Cut asparagus into inch lengths if preferred.

### Macaroni in Milk

Heat 1 qt. of milk in inner cup of double boiler, add 1 cup of macaroni and cook until tender, perhaps for 2 hrs. Serve plain as side dish or for luncheon or supper. It may also be served with stewed raisins, with or without cream.

## ★ Cream Mold of Macaroni

Cook ½ cup of macaroni with or without a few slices of onion and a suspicion of garlic, in 2 cups of water with ½ tablespn. of butter until tender and well dried out; drain, add ⅔ cup milk, 1 large egg and salt. Turn into well buttered mold and bake covered in pan of water in moderate oven until egg is set, ¾–1 hour. Serve with Boundary Castle or any suitable sauce.

## ★ Macaroni—Sour Cream

2–3 cups macaroni
1 pt. sour cream (or sour milk with butter or oil)
1 teaspn. salt
1 egg

Add beaten egg and salt to cream and pour over cooked macaroni in baking dish; sprinkle with crumbs and bake until egg is set.

Rice may be used in place of macaroni, tomato also may be added sometimes with chopped onion; a delicate flavoring of sage gives another variety.

# BREADS—LEAVENED

## Yeast

Yeast is a plant and success in bread-making depends upon its growth.

Plants require warmth, food and moisture and thrive the best when not too warm nor too cold.

A temperature of from 75 degrees to not over 90 degrees is the most favorable for the growth of the yeast plant.

Compressed yeast is the most convenient to use when it can be obtained fresh, but the bread made from it lacks the sweet rich flavor of that made from a good soft yeast; so from the great number of good recipes for liquid yeast I give two with which I have had excellent success.

Use only mature, well ripened potatoes for yeast. Hops may be omitted but the yeast keeps better and the bread is lighter and sweeter when a few are used.

Keep yeast in several small jars rather than in one large one, so as not to disturb the whole when using from it.

Bread rises slowly from yeast that is less than 48 hours old. When liquid yeast is used, let it count as part of the wetting. Compressed yeast is meant when dry is not specified in recipes calling for cakes of yeast.

To use compressed yeast, slice it in rather thin slices, sprinkle sugar between the layers and pour just enough lukewarm water over it to moisten the sugar, not enough to cover the yeast. Let stand until foamy and use at once.

One cake of compressed yeast equals 4 tablespns. of either grated or mashed potato yeast.

## Grated Potato Yeast

2 qts. water

2 tablespns. hops

6 medium sized or 3 very large potatoes

½ cup sugar

¼ cup salt

1 cup soft yeast, or 2 cakes of good dry yeast (yeast foam when obtainable)

Dissolve yeast in warm water with part of the sugar. Simmer the hops in water for half an hour, strain, add enough water to make 2 qts. and keep at boiling point. Put sugar and salt into a large granite or porcelain kettle, quickly grate the pared potatoes over them, set the kettle over the fire and pour the boiling hop water on to the mixture, stirring; let boil until thickened, remove from fire, cool to lukewarm, add the yeast, beating it in well and let stand on table or shelf in warm kitchen; as it rises, stir it down once in a while; when well risen, set in a cool place and stir down occasionally until it does not rise any more. Fill clean cold jars about ⅔ full and when settled, fasten covers on and put in ice box.

Use 1 tablespn. of yeast to each pint of water when setting bread over night, and double the quantity for starting in the morning.

## Mashed Potato Yeast

1¼ cup smooth mashed potato

1 tablespn. loose hops

1 tablespn. sugar

1 teaspn. salt

¾ cup of water in which potatoes and hops were boiled, 1 cake of dry yeast dissolved in ¼ cup of water with a little of the sugar, or, ½ cup of hop water and ½ cup of liquid yeast.

Tie the hops in a piece of cheese cloth and cook with the well washed but not pared potatoes (the yeast is lighter if the skins are left on); when done, drain and peel potatoes and rub through colander on to the salt and sugar; beat well, pour water on gradually, add yeast, beat, put into a clean glass jar, lay the cover on without fastening down and let stand in a warm room until full of bubbles, no longer; then set in a cold place. When thoroughly cooled, fasten the cover tight and keep in refrigerator.

Use ¼–½ cup of yeast to a pint of liquid, according to the time you wish to give the bread to rise.

## Dry Yeast

1 cup loose hops
2 qts. water
1 qt. pared potatoes in small pieces
flour
1 cup corn meal

Boil potatoes with hops tied in cheese cloth until tender; remove hops (squeezing bag when cool), put potatoes and water through colander, and stir into the liquid while scalding hot, enough flour to make a rather stiff batter. Beat well, add ½ cup of yeast or 2 dry yeast cakes dissolved in water. When light, add the cup of corn meal or enough to make a dough stiff enough to roll; roll ⅓–½ in. thick, cut into small square or round cakes, dry in the sun or in a slightly warm oven (they are sometimes dried between two boards covered with corn meal) until so much of the moisture is expelled that they cannot ferment.

If kept dry the cakes will retain their strength for a long time. The small pieces of dough may be crumbled and dried.

## Flour

White, graham and whole wheat are the flours most commonly used in making bread. White *bread* flour is made from spring wheat, which is richer in gluten than winter wheat and is of a rich cream color.

Winter wheat flour is more suitable for cakes and pastry, and for that reason is called *pastry* flour.

A blended flour, spring and winter wheat combined, is considered by some the most nearly perfect bread flour.

Graham flour is composed of the whole kernel of the wheat, its bran overcoat and all, ground up together. The bran contains no nutriment and is irritating to some stomachs. Graham flour is nearly always made from winter wheat.

In making whole wheat or entire wheat flour, the bran or fibrous covering of the kernel is removed and the entire nourishing part of the grain is ground. Whole wheat flour is usually made from spring wheat.

Some so-called "whole wheat" flours are simply very fine graham; that is, the bran is all there, but ground very fine.

The best grades of flour are the cheapest as a smaller quantity is required for the same amount of liquid. Good flour also requires less kneading.

Perhaps the greatest deception has been practised in "gluten" flours. Some which have been advertised as pure gluten have been found to contain as high as 63 and 75 per cent. of starch. A pure gluten flour for making yeast bread is out of the question.

Flour made from new wheat will for a time improve with age, but after a certain period it begins to deteriorate; so it is not best to lay in a too large supply at once.

Keep flour in a warm, dry place, as all bread, cakes and pastry are lighter made from dry flour.

"For use in bread-making the superfine white flour is not the best. Its use is neither healthful nor economical. Fine flour bread is lacking in nutritive elements to be found in bread made from the whole wheat. It is a frequent cause of constipation and other unhealthful conditions."

## BREAD—YEAST

### Suggestions

Bread should not be set over night when there is the least possibility of its becoming light enough to fall before it can be attended to in the morning.

Dough mixed stiff at first requires double the quantity of yeast of that started with a sponge, but as this method has several advantages it is becoming the favorite. Beat the batter very thoroughly for either method, as that has much to do with the lightness of the bread.

Keep bread at all stages at as even a temperature as possible and away from draughts of air. A large pasteboard box is an excellent thing to set it into.

A moist atmosphere is most favorable for raising bread.

Keep bread covered close to prevent a crust from forming over the top. Paper is better than cloth to exclude the air.

To hasten the rising of bread, use a larger quantity of yeast rather than a higher temperature. Above 90 degrees the bacteria which were in the flour or yeast may begin to grow and the bread will be sour. Given more time and raised at a lower temperature, bread will be sweeter and of a finer texture.

Attend to bread at every stage as soon as light, before it begins to fall; exercise especial care in this respect with compressed yeast as it loses its life very quickly after becoming light.

Bread will rise better in a deep vessel, such as a pail or a stone crock, than in a broad flat pan. Always oil the dishes used for raising it in.

Each time that bread rises it loses some of its sweetness and nutritive value, so the fewer times it is allowed to rise the better, if light enough to be digestible.

Some cooks prefer flour that has been delicately browned for setting the sponge for bread.

A good bread kneader is one of the best investments in cooking utensils. It saves time and strength and makes better bread.

"In the making of raised or yeast bread, milk should not be used in place of water. The use of milk is an additional expense and it makes the bread much less wholesome. Milk bread does not keep sweet so long after baking as does that made with water and it ferments more readily in the stomach."

In cakes and crusts where milk is used with yeast, sour milk may be substituted for sweet with the same results.

To aid fermentation, a little sugar may be used in starting bread, but not enough to cover the sweet taste of the flour.

At a great altitude, bread rises very quickly; and requires less yeast.

Do not allow bread to get over light, even if it does not become sour; for the sweet taste will be destroyed, and if in the loaf, it will fall in the oven.

Whole wheat and graham bread will be lighter if ⅓ white flour is used; and if white flour alone is used for the sponge the bread will not be so apt to sour.

Whole wheat and graham bread need to be mixed stiffer than white and must not be allowed to become very light or they will fall in the oven and have a hollow place in the loaf.

Bread from whole wheat and graham flour requires slower and longer baking.

Whole wheat, graham or rye bread may be steamed 3 hours and baked slowly ½ hr., sometimes.

Salt delays fermentation, so when bread is started with a sponge the salt should not be added until the sponge is light, and it may be worked in at the end of the first rising of the mass of dough.

When a large quantity of bread is made at a time, a smaller proportion of yeast is required. Stir soft yeast well before using from it. Do not let the jar of yeast stand in a warm kitchen for a few minutes even.

It is impossible to give an exact rule for the proportion of flour to liquid in bread as different brands of flour vary and the same brand may be dryer or more moist at different times; but usually not less than three times as much flour as of liquid is required, and not much more.

Near the sea level bread dough may be mixed as soft as it can be well handled; but as the altitude increases the stiffness of the dough should increase.

Flour must be warm when added to bread at any stage.

Do not add any flour to bread after the last rising before putting it into the tins, "as all the flour in it is, in a fermentative sense, cooked and the addition of raw flour injures its quality."—*Charles Cristodoro.* Oil the board and your hands instead.

"Bread should be light and sweet, not the least taint of sourness should be tolerated. The loaves should be small and so thoroughly baked that so far as possible, the yeast germs shall be destroyed. When hot or new, raised bread of any kind is difficult of digestion. *It should never appear on the table.*"

The loaves should be baked in separate tins, brick shaped ones being best. If the loaf feels soft on the sides when removed from the tin, return it to the oven for it is not done. When done, leave loaves where the air can circulate around them until cool.

Keep bread in tin or stone receptacles, never in wood; wash them often in warm soapsuds and scald thoroughly.

Never cover bread in the box with a cloth, if anything is required, use paper. Cloth causes a musty taste and smell.

Do not allow crumbs or bits of bread to collect in the box or jar.

To freshen stale bread or buns, place them in a hot oven above a pan of boiling water; or put into one tin and cover with another and leave 10–30 m. according to size of loaf and heat of oven.

Rolls are sometimes dipped in milk or water and heated in the oven; or, put into a paper sack and left in the oven for 10 m.

## White Bread

2–4 tablespns. liquid yeast, or 1 cake compressed yeast

warm water to make 1 qt. of liquid

2 tablespns. oil

1 teaspn. sugar

1 teaspn. salt

3–3½ qts. flour

Put yeast in a quart measure (compressed yeast will have been dissolved according to directions) and fill the measure with warm water. Turn into warm mixing bowl, add oil, sugar and salt (sugar may be omitted), mingle, add flour until a drop batter is formed; beat vigorously for 5 m., then continue to add flour. When too stiff to stir, knead on molding board until dough is smooth and does not stick to the board by deft handling, place in a well oiled deep dish, cover well and let stand in a moderately warm place until light. It may now be folded down and turned over and allowed to come up half way again, or be put at once into the tins.

Allow bread to rise in tins to a little more than double its bulk (experience will do more for one in determining the proper degree of lightness than any recipe), and put into a moderate oven with spaces between the pans; when well risen and moderately browned, lower the temperature of the oven a little and finish baking. Cover with asbestos sheets or paper if bread is in danger of becoming too brown. ¾–1 hr. will be required for baking a medium sized loaf.

## Fruit Bread

Use double the quantity of oil and from ¼–½ cup of sugar in the recipe for white bread, add 2 large cups of seedless raisins or 1 cup each of raisins and currants. Dates or figs may be used when preferred.

## Nut Bread

Use 2 cups coarse chopped nuts instead of fruit, in fruit bread recipe. Brown sugar may be used instead of white, or sugar may be omitted altogether.

## Irish Bread

Brown sugar, raisins, currants and caraway seeds in fruit bread recipe.

## Whole Wheat and Graham Bread

Use ⅓ white flour and ⅔ whole wheat or graham instead of all white flour in the recipe for white bread. These breads require to be kneaded a little stiffer than white flour bread to prevent their being coarse grained and falling in the oven; also, care must be taken that they do not get too light before baking. It is a mistake to put molasses or sugar into graham bread as it conceals the sweet nutty flavor of the flour.

## Zwieback Bread

1 pt. water
½ teaspn. salt
4 tablespns. yeast or
1 cake compressed yeast
⅓–½ cup corn meal
white flour to knead

It is better not to use oil in zwieback bread.

## New York "Home Made" Bread

2–4 tablespns. liquid yeast or 1 cake compressed yeast, warm water to make 1 qt., white flour for drop batter; beat well. When light, add 1 cup corn meal gruel (to make, use 1 tablespn. of granular meal to each cup of boiling water and cook 2 hrs.), 1¼ teaspn. salt, and flour for smooth dough. Let rise in bulk once, then put into pans. A baker gave me this idea. He said he had a great run on it once in New York City under the name of "Home Made" bread. The bread is very moist and sweet.

### Oatmeal Bread. Mrs. Cobb, Bay City

¾ cup oatmeal or 1 cup (pressed down) of rolled oats
1 qt. water
2 tablespns. oil
¼ cup sugar
2–4 tablespns. yeast or 1 cake compressed yeast
1 teaspn. salt
white flour

Cook oats in water as for porridge, 1½–3 hrs., cool to lukewarm, add sugar, oil, yeast, and flour for sponge; beat, let rise, add salt, and flour for soft dough; when risen form into loaves and when moderately light bake from ¾–1 hr. Sugar need not be used.

### ★ Rye Bread

1 pt. water
1 tablespn. oil
¾ teaspn. salt
3 tablespns. liquid yeast
3 cups rye meal, not flour
4½–5 cups white flour or enough to make a very stiff dough

Let rise once in bulk and put into tins; when light, bake in moderate oven. Add caraway seeds when liked.

## ★ Rice Bread

Cook 2 cups of rice in 2 qts. of water until tender; cool to lukewarm; add 4–6 tablespns. yeast with water to make 1 pt., 1½ teaspn. salt and 4–5 cups white flour, or enough to make a very stiff dough.

## ★ Crisp Bread

*Sponge*:—

    1 cup water
    1 tablespn. oil
    ⅓ cake yeast
    1½–1¾ cup bread flour

When light, add 1 cup fine dry bread crumbs, knead well, use crumbs to roll the dough, roll ¼ in. thick, cut into large rings, let rise and bake in moderate oven until crisp.

Crumbs may be kneaded into bread dough and finished the same.

## Potato Ball Bread

    2 cups mashed potato
    1 cake dry yeast
    1 teaspn. salt
    2 teaspns. sugar

Add yeast cake powdered fine, to the potato when lukewarm, and the salt and sugar when cold; form into a ball, cover and keep in cool place 2 or 3 days. When ready to bake, add 2 cups mashed potato mixed with 1 teaspn. salt and 2 of sugar to the ball. Make a ball of half the mixture and add enough warm water to the remainder to make 2 qts. or more. Add warm flour to knead, let rise in bulk once or twice before putting into pans.

Proceed in the same manner for each baking, keeping the ball covered in a cool place between bakings. A new ball will not need to be started oftener than once in three months if at all.

This yeast works very quickly and makes beautiful bread. Of course for small bakings, half the quantity of yeast would be sufficient.

### "Delicious" Bread

I do not know the origin of this yeast but the bread is truly named.

Put into a pitcher or some suitable deep vessel 2 cups of mashed potato to which has been added 1 cup of sugar and 1 qt. of warm water. Cover and let stand in a warm room for from 1 to 3 days or until covered with a foam almost like the meringue on a pie. Mix some of this foam with 1 cup of warm mashed potato, let stand in a warm place 1–2 hrs., add 1 tablespn. of salt and set away in a cool place.

To the original yeast add 1–2 qts. water, 2–3 teaspns. salt and warm flour to knead; when light, stir down, and put into pans the second time it rises. Be careful not to let it get over light in the pans before baking.

For the next baking, add 1 cup of sugar and the 1 cup of potato reserved from the last baking, to 2 cups of fresh mashed potato; take out 1 cupful as before, let stand in warm place 1 hr., add 1 tablespn. of salt and set in a cool place.

To the 2 cups of potato add a little water and set in a warm place until light, when water to make 2 or 3 qts. may be added and the bread kneaded up.

This bread needs to be eaten to be appreciated.

The yeast may be used in universal crust, raised cakes and wherever other yeast is used, with delightful results.

### Boston Brown Bread. Corn and Rye

1 pt. warm water
1 tablespn. oil
1 teaspn. salt
¾ cup molasses
⅔–1 cake of yeast
1 pt. rye meal
1 pt. granular corn meal

Mix all ingredients, let rise; pour into tins, let rise, not too light; steam 3 hrs. bake 20–30 m. in slow oven.

Raisins or nuts or both are good in brown bread.

### Boston Brown Bread, No. 2.

1 pt. water
1 tablespn. oil
¾ cup molasses
⅔–1 cake yeast
1 teaspn. salt
1⅓ cup pastry flour
1⅓ cup rye flour
3–3⅓ cups granular corn meal

Mix all ingredients except corn meal, let rise, add meal, turn into tins and when risen not quite double, steam for 3 hrs. and bake 20 m. to ½ hr. in slow oven.

## West Virginia Scalded Corn Meal Bread

1 cup Rhode Island meal
1 cup boiling water
1½ cup warm water
3–3½ cups dry meal
¾ cake of compressed yeast
1 small egg
1–1¼ teaspn. salt
1 tablespn. oil

A little more meal may be used.

Scald 1 cup of meal with boiling water, add warm water, yeast, oil and dry meal. When light, add salt and beaten egg, let rise in the dish in which it is to be baked. The bread is best baked in an iron skillet or frying pan with a cover.

## ★ Corn Cake

*Sponge—*

1 pt. skimmed milk
1 tablespn. oil
1 tablespn. sugar
½ cake yeast
4¼–4½ cups pastry flour

When light; 1 teaspn. salt, 2 cups granular corn meal, 2 eggs slightly beaten. Turn into well oiled pan to depth of 1–1½ in., let stand in warm place a few minutes, bake in moderate oven.

The quantity of flour will vary with the brand, 3¾–4 cups only of bread flour will be required. The eggs make a finer grained as well as lighter bread. One egg will do if eggs are scarce.

## Salt Rising Bread—Suggestions

Tastes and opinions differ concerning this bread but no other takes its place to those who were accustomed to it in childhood.

With a little practice, salt rising bread becomes less work to make than hop yeast bread. It is more wholesome and richer flavored and keeps better than other yeast bread, and it has a fine cake-like texture.

The experience of some persons is that salt rising bread is less apt to cause acidity in the stomach than hop yeast bread.

The secrets of success with it are in keeping it evenly warm; in not making it too stiff; and in not kneading it too much. Too much flour renders salt rising bread dry and powdery.

The water surrounding the rising at different stages should be at a temperature of 110 to 125 degrees, or so that it feels hot to the hand, but not scalding.

In cold weather, an ideal way to keep the loaves warm while rising is to put them on bricks in a pan or tub of warm water and cover them with a blanket.

It is well to scald all utensils used for the bread with boiling sal-soda water and to use the same water to stand the yeast in while rising.

While the flour added to salt rising bread should be warm, it must never have been hot at any time before using as it is the yeast germs which it and the other ingredients contain that raise the bread.

The loaves should be wrapped in a thick cloth when taken from the oven and left until cold. Salt rising bread makes sweet and tender zwieback.

### Salt Rising Bread. No. 1

Mix 1 tablespn. each of salt, sugar and corn meal (white or Rhode Island if obtainable) with 3 tablespns. of oil, pour over all 1½ pt. of boiling water; stir until sugar and salt are dissolved, then add 1½ pt. cold water that has never been heated. Add warm flour for thick batter which will be rather thin after beating (about 2 qts., perhaps). Beat thoroughly and set in pan of water at 110 to 125 degrees or in some place that can be kept at a uniform temperature much warmer than for common yeast bread but not warm enough to scald the rising. When the first bubbles appear, beat the batter thoroughly and repeat the beating each hour until light, which will be in from 4–6 hours. The rising should not be allowed to become too light at any time. When the batter is light, close the doors so that there will be no draughts. Have the pans oiled and warm, and the flour warm. Add the flour rapidly with very little stirring, to the batter; when stiff enough, turn all out on to a warmed, floured board and work in quickly with as little kneading as possible enough flour for a rather soft dough; form into loaves and place in oiled pans, set in a warm place, covering well to keep a crust from forming over the top as well as to keep the loaves warm. As soon as light, place in a moderate oven and bake thoroughly.

### Salt Rising Bread. No. 2

To 1 cup very warm water add ½ teaspn. of salt and fine middlings (shorts) to make a rather stiff batter; beat well, cover and set in a dish of very warm water, covered, beat 2 or 3 times while rising. When light, turn into a warm mixing bowl, add 1 pt. or more of warm water, a little more salt and warm graham flour (part white flour if preferred) for a soft dough, and finish the same as No. 1.

## ★ Universal Crust

For shortcakes, fruit tarts, meat and vegetable pies, pot pie dumplings, crackers, buns, steamed puddings, loaf cake, doughnuts and cookies, rusk and Sally Lunn.

> 1 cup skimmed milk
> ⅓ cup (large 4 tablespns.) oil
> ¼ teaspn. salt
> ½ teaspn. sugar
> 1–2 tablespns. liquid yeast or ⅓ cake compressed yeast
> pastry flour

Mix all ingredients except salt and add flour for sponge batter; beat; when light, add salt and warm flour for moderately stiff dough. Knead a little and cut into biscuit for the top of fruit tarts or meat or vegetable pies, or place on tins for shortcake crusts. For dumplings, use only ¼ cup of oil or 1½ tablespn. of raw nut butter.

The crust may be kneaded stiff at first and allowed to rise twice.

If the crusts are not fine grained it is because you have not used enough flour or have not kneaded them enough; but they do not want to be quite as stiff as bread is usually mixed.

Shortcake crusts or tins of thin biscuit may be made and kept on hand and just warmed up when needed, or laid over meat or vegetable pie fillings or hot cooked fruit fillings and left in the oven long enough to warm through.

We consider this one of the most valuable recipes in the book since it can be used in so many ways in the place of baking powder crusts.

### Sour Cream Crust—no soda

1 cup thick sour cream
⅓–½ cake compressed yeast
¼ teaspn. salt
white flour

Make sponge or knead at once to soft dough, let rise, make into any desired shape and when light, bake. This is very nice for shortcake crusts and can be used for nearly all purposes that universal crust is. That the cream was sour would not be known after the crust is baked.

### Sally Lunn. Breakfast or Supper Bread

Use 1 egg, with or without 1 tablespn. of sugar to each cup of milk in universal crust. Bake in shallow or thick loaf as preferred.

www.ingramcontent.com/pod-product-compliance
Lightning Source LLC
Chambersburg PA
CBHW081122080526
44587CB00021B/3707

www.ingramcontent.com/pod-product-compliance
Lightning Source LLC
Chambersburg PA
CBHW081122080526
44587CB00021B/3707